# The
# Parenting
# Crisis

# The Parenting Crisis

## Parenting Today's Teenagers

Dr. Scott Wooding

Fitzhenry & Whiteside

The Parenting Crisis
Copyright © 2005 by Dr. Scott Wooding

Published in Canada by
Fitzhenry & Whiteside
195 Allstate Parkway
Markham, Ontario L3R 4T8

Published in the United States by
Fitzhenry & Whiteside
121 Harvard Avenue, Suite 2
Allston, Massachusetts 02134

1 3 5 7 9 10 8 6 4 2

**Library and Archives Canada Cataloguing in Publication**

Wooding, G. Scott, (Gary Scott), 1944-
  The parenting crisis / G. Scott Wooding.
Includes index.
ISBN 1-55041-843-2
  1. Parenting.  2. Parent and teenager.  I. Title.
HQ799.15.W658 2005        649'.125        C2005-900468-1

**U.S. Publisher Cataloguing-in-Publication Data
(Library of Congress Standards)**

Wooding, G. Scott.
  The parenting crisis / G. Scott Wooding.
[320] p. :  cm.
Includes index.
Summary: An advice book for parents dealing with teenagers, who are showing the effects of stress in both their health and in their everyday behaviour.
ISBN 1-55041-843-2   (pbk.)
1. Parenting.  2. Parent and teenager.  3. Teenagers.  4. Stress in adolescence.  I. Title.
649.125 22   HQ799.15W55  2005

Fitzhenry & Whiteside acknowledges with thanks the Canada Council for the Arts, the Government of Canada through the Book Publishing Industry Development Program (BPIDP), and the Ontario Arts Council for their support of our publishing program.

Printed in Canada
Text design by Darrell McCalla
Cover design by Tania Craan
Cover image © Getty Images

# Contents

# Introduction

This book has been somewhat longer in arriving than was originally planned. Its genesis lay in the growing concern of my therapist colleagues and me over the effects of divorce on young children. Unfortunately, while there was ample anecdotal evidence to suggest that divorce was very hard on children, the research evidence had not yet caught up. Divorce was only liberalized in the late 1960s, and it took the better part of two generations before its effects could be clearly seen. By this time, other pressures on children were compounding the negative effects of divorce. It was becoming increasingly obvious, from statistics on youth crime, drug and alcohol use, and mental illness, that children were under more pressure than ever before. Parents were reporting more and more problems raising their children, but did not know why they were having these problems. It was clear that the time had come to explore the causes of these problems and to find some solutions.

I wrote this book, then, to explain to parents how different stressors in modern society are resulting in the very high youth crime rate, the even higher drug and alcohol use by our young people, and very high incidences of depression and anxiety in this population. The idea is to educate parents, not to frighten them or to chastise them. The problems in our society that are creating this youth stress have developed gradually and insidiously. Often they have resulted when solutions to one problem in society inadvertently caused a problem in another area. The clearest example of this is the effectiveness of the second wave of the women's movement in the 1970s. By redressing the inequalities in the treatment of the sexes, mothers left their homes for the workplace. This meant they had to place their children in childcare for the whole day, which meant that the children grew up with neither the close parental bonding of earlier generations nor the parental role models for teaching values and discipline, the absence of which exacerbated the higher levels of stress discussed above.

While such problems are no one's fault, they must be brought to society's attention so that solutions can be found before they become too deeply rooted. Parenting skills are mostly learned from our own parents and if nothing is done about today's parenting situation, the next generation will only continue the mistakes of the present one.

Throughout this book it may often seem that I am pointing fingers at modern parents for being selfish, greedy, or careless. Nothing could be further from the truth. Most parents today care deeply about the welfare of their children and are doing the best they can in a very complex society. Unfortunately they are often consumed by their own careers and confounded by the absence of clear information about parenting, leaving them with a stark inability to make informed and common-sense decisions about their families.

This book, then, seeks to raise awareness of the effects of modern social changes on children and to help parents make changes in their own families that will reduce the stress on their kids. We need a return to the simpler lives that were evident just a generation or two ago. We need to reject some of the values that have crept into our lives and put more emphasis on the welfare of our children and our families. What has been lost in the past few years can quickly be regained if parents become aware of the damage their lifestyles are inadvertently causing their children. Otherwise there truly will be a "parenting crisis."

This book is meant to be a practical, hands-on book for parents and educators. The problems discussed are real problems that have been evident in my many years as a counselor and therapist. The solutions presented are real, plausible solutions that all parents and educators can take hold of. And, more important, they are based on the growing body of research from leading medical doctors, psychologists, educators, and others. To avoid distracting readers from the main points, however, I have avoided filling the text with endless citations to the many research studies quoted. Instead, I placed all of the references into a single listing at the back of the book.

# CHAPTER I

# The Crisis

O ur children and teenagers are under more stress today than ever before. While most adults have learned to deal with stress, our children have not. Many of the childhood and teenage problems that have surfaced in the past decade are the result of these high stress levels. And parenting methods seem to be at the root of much of the stress our children are feeling.

This book explores the connections between parenting problems and stress in children. It seeks to help parents understand where things are going wrong and what the impact is on their children. More important, it offers parents concrete suggestions on how to put their parenting in the right direction, thus helping their children to grow up in a healthy and happy environment.

## Stress in Our Youth

That stress in today's young people is reaching unprecedented levels is supported by many sources.

- One-third of American teens are stressed out on a daily basis and two-thirds are stressed at least once a week, according to a 1999 University of Michigan study of more than 8000 high school students.

- In 2002, 70 percent of students in Marlborough High School in Massachusetts reported that they were stressed out.

• In 2003, 38 percent of Ontario students reported being constantly under stress, while 29 percent indicated that they lost sleep due to worrying. This represented an almost 4 percent increase in stress levels from 2001.

Why do these figures matter? Why should we be concerned about this increase in youth stress? Because stress takes an incredible toll on the human mind and body. For children whose minds

## The Stress Response

Dr. Hans Selye, the father of stress research, defined stress as "the non-specific response of the body to any demand." Selye and a number of later researchers showed that this "nonspecific response" is displayed by a wide variety of reactions that comprise psycho-physiological arousal. This arousal results from actions of the sympathetic nervous system and involves the release of about 20 hormones, including catecholamines (such as adrenaline and noradrenaline) and glucocorticoids (such as cortisol). Originating from the adrenal glands, located just above the kidneys, these stimulants help the body cope with the cause of the arousal, by releasing stored sugar from the liver into the bloodstream for extra muscle fuel, by increasing heart rate and respiration, increasing blood pressure, fighting off inflammation, and enhancing muscle tension.

Once the crisis is over, the parasympathetic nervous system initiates a series of actions to return the body to its normal, relaxed state. These measures help reverse the effects of stress in our body, by decreasing the heart rate, releasing stress-inducing chemicals (such as adrenaline and cortisol) from the tissues, and decreasing blood pressure. They also result in a growing sense of ease or a calmness in the mind.

Originally, the stress response evolved as a "fight or flight" response to physical danger, an automatic defence system to help our ancestors fight predators or run away from them. Today, we are unlikely to be attacked by a woolly mammoth or another predator that puts us in physical danger. Modern stressors tend to be more social and emotional—relationships, work, school—or even technological. Though less physically dangerous, these modern stressors are more prevalent. In fact, our society has become so frantic that our sympathetic system is continuously triggered, and our parasympathetic system rarely has time to recover and allow us to calm down. During these long periods of high stress, the body stays in an almost constant state of arousal, and the anti-stress parasympathetic response simply cannot keep up. The body is not designed to live in this continual state of stress. If not given enough time to recover, serious damage to both the body and the mind can result.

and bodies are still developing, the impact of stress is even more dramatic.

Adults are well aware that stress can increase their risk of heart attack and stroke and cause depression. Unfortunately, very few people realize that the high levels of stress being experienced by our children are manifesting themselves in equally dangerous symptoms.

## Aggression and Violence

One of the most obvious signs of stress is the tendency to get angry quickly. Most adults have learned to restrict their reactions of anger to verbal jibes, but kids, and especially teenagers, lack adult controls and are liable to lash out at others when they're stressed. This lashing out often results in violence, usually towards members of their peer group, but often towards parents as well. The violence takes the form of physical fighting, bullying, dating violence and date rape, and even homicide. The evidence supporting a trend towards increased teenage violence is compelling.

In response to the tragedy at Columbine High School in Colorado in 1999, the United States Office of the Surgeon General examined the prevalence of violence among young people. The study, published in 2001, found that many indicators of youth violence, such as homicide, declined after 1993, but others increased. Rates of arrest for aggravated assault were 70 percent higher, for example. The report concluded: "Even though youth violence is less lethal today than it was in 1993, the percentage of adolescents involved in violent behavior remains alarmingly high."

Other research reinforced the Surgeon General's concern. A 1999 study by the Centers for Disease Control and Prevention found that more than 1 in 3 students had been in a physical fight in the previous year and that 1 in 9 had been hurt badly enough to need medical treatment. Furthermore, 1 in 4 male high school students said they carried a weapon in the past month. These figures included 5 percent who reported carrying a gun. When asked why they carry weapons to school, students typically answered "for protection." In other words, they carried a gun not with the intention of attacking someone, but to defend themselves from attackers.

Physical fighting among young men has been present for many generations. What is new is the violence and aggression now being seen in young women. Between 1988 and 1998 the arrest rate in Canada for interpersonal offences increased twice as fast for female youth (+127 percent) as for their male youth (+65 percent). In the United States, the male-female violence ratio, as measured by arrest statistics and violence surveys, was 10 to 1 a generation ago. Today, that ratio stands at 4 to 1. These figures are also reflected in the schools where the number of girls suspended or expelled for fighting has risen dramatically.

While the reasons for this alarming increase in adolescent female violence are not fully known, we can point to several factors. Some authorities feel that the same factors that are keeping male violence at very high levels are now affecting young women as well: high stress levels produced by family breakups, lower attendance at church, less involvement in the community, and higher pressures in school. Other experts point to the female role models portrayed in the media. Buffy the Vampire Slayer and Lara Croft are shown as capable of incredible violence. Their good looks, confidence, and physical prowess make them role models for female adolescents, who may emulate this violence in their own lives. Most likely, a combination of factors is causing the increase in female violence statistics. But there can be little doubt that higher stress in the lives of young women is playing a key role.

Another major area of concern about violence and aggression in the adolescent population is dating violence. A 2001 Youth Risk Survey in Massachusetts indicated that at least 1 in 4 teenagers was involved in violent relationships. Another study in the same year, conducted by the *Journal of the American Medical Association*, showed that 20 percent of female high school students reported being physically or sexually abused by their dating partners. An even more frightening study was published in 1996 in the *American Journal of Preventive Medicine*. It showed that 25 percent of students in Grades 8 and 9 reported non-sexual dating violence, while 8 percent had been victims of sexual dating violence. These are kids in the 13 to 15 age range. While some research shows that dating violence is not a new phenomenon, what is disturbing is that the victims are getting younger and younger.

Teenage aggression also displays itself in bullying. This behavior can range from verbal assaults (such as teasing or taunting among boys or spreading rumors or gossip among girls) to actual physical contact (such as hitting, slapping, or pushing). In recent years a new form of bullying has appeared—cyber-bullying, which involves threats and taunts over the Internet. What about the anti-bullying programs established in many schools after the massacre of high school students in 1999? If they had been effective, we should have seen a decrease in bullying behavior. This has not been the case.

Figures collected by the National Center for Education Studies showed that bullying in American schools actually increased 5 percent from 1999 to 2001. More recent research shows that up to 80 percent of students report being bullied at some time during their school years. This research also shows that one-third of parents fear for their children's physical safety when they're at school, with the figures higher for parents of children in upper grades. That bullying is prevalent and even growing in our schools, despite the anti-bullying campaigns, can only mean that education alone is not enough.

## Psychological Distress

The high stress levels that lead to violence and aggression can also lead to psychological problems, such as depression, anxiety disorders, and eating disorders. The symptoms of these conditions in teenagers are very difficult for parents (and sometimes even professionals) to diagnose until they reach an acute stage. For some, this is too late.

Researchers have shown that stress produces measurable changes in the brain chemistry and that leads to a depressed mood. According to the United States National Institute of Mental Health, 1 in 8 adolescents may suffer from depression, and of these, almost 5 percent are classified as having major depression. Australian research shows that, at some time during their adolescence, almost one-quarter of teenagers will suffer a major depressive episode, which means that at least five of the symptoms of depression last for at least two weeks. Major depressive episodes are obviously the most dangerous because they can lead to suicide, but even when they do not, they can create problems later in life. Adults who experienced even a single bout of a major depressive disorder in adolescence are likely to demonstrate pervasive psychosocial impairment, according to research by psychologist Peter Lewinsohn of the Oregon Research Institute.

It's difficult to diagnose depression in children and teenagers because their symptoms are frequently different than in adults. For example, teenagers are often irritable and angry when they're depressed, and parents often interpret these symptoms as normal teenage rebellion and moodiness. But statistics do show very high levels of depression in the adolescent population and that depression is occurring earlier in adolescent life than it did in past decades.

Perhaps the best indicator of depression levels is suicide figures. In the past 25 years, while the general incidence of suicide has decreased, the suicide rate in the 15 to 24 age range has tripled, making suicide the third leading cause of death in adolescents. Of even greater concern, the United States Centers for Disease Control indicated that, from 1980 to 1997, the rate of suicide among 15- to 19-year-olds increased by 11 percent, but among 10- to 14-year-olds it increased a startling 109 percent.

## Depression in a 10-Year-Old

Riley, a 10-year-old girl, was brought to the author by her mother. School authorities had discovered Riley crying alone in the schoolyard during recess, and her journal writings confirmed her extreme sadness.

Riley's parents were going through a bitter custody battle. Her father was petitioning the court for more access. Her mother was resisting the petition. She did not think the father, who had a history of drinking and drug use, should see Riley more than every other weekend, as their agreement allowed. The father insisted that a psychologist be called in to do a bilateral assessment, which would determine which parent was the fittest to raise Riley.

In the course of their dispute, both parents were saying angry things about each other and making bitter accusations. This is what was making Riley feel depressed. Despite the fact that her parents could not get along with each other, she loved both of them. She was satisfied with the custodial arrangements and did not understand why they needed to be changed. She felt that she was being forced to take sides – something she did not feel able to do.

A 2003 study by Ontario's Centre for Addiction and Mental Health indicated that 12 percent of the students surveyed had considered suicide in the past year, up from 10 percent just two years previously. This is a frighteningly high statistic. Since suicide doesn't happen without depression, these figures indicate that depression must be on the rise in young people.

Stress causes not only depression, but also anxiety disorders, such as panic attacks, agoraphobia, social phobia, and generalized anxiety disorder. In the past, these were disorders of adults, but they have begun appearing recently in the younger generation. According to the U.S. Department of Health and Human Services, as many as 13 percent of young people ranging from 9 to 17 may have anxiety disorders. Symptoms include shortness of breath, palpitations, chest pains, choking or smothering sensations, and fear of "going crazy" or losing control. Anxiety in children and teenagers manifests itself as repeated school absences or an inability to finish school, impaired relations with peers, low self-esteem, alcohol or other drug use, problems adjusting to work situations, and anxiety disorders in adulthood.

Adolescents themselves do not always know what causes them to behave this way. They usually do not realize that stress and anxiety are the root of their problems. That usually means that the symptoms are treated rather than the actual cause. If school absences are the problem, parents might ground their child for a few weeks. If drug and alcohol use is the problem, then similar consequences might be used, or the teenager might be sent to an addiction counselor. Both of these approaches blame the child for the problem, and that can worsen the situation, especially if the anxiety was rooted in a negative home situation. Perhaps the parents are estranged, or custody battles are in progress, or step-parents enter a family, or more innocuously— the child is involved in too many extracurricular activities. It often takes a counselor with experience with teens to diagnose the cause and then parents with open minds to help find a solution.

## Drug and Alcohol Use

Much of adolescent drug and alcohol use might be attributed to normal risk taking and experimental behavior. Yet the statistics on drug and alcohol use among adolescents are too high to blame on experimentation alone. It seems likely that young people, like many adults, are using drugs and alcohol to reduce the effects of stress.

Historical reviews of drug use indicate that the figures were highest in the late 1970s. When research began to show many serious problems associated with drug use, particularly LSD and amphetamines, the schools initiated drug education programs. The result was a steady decline in drug use among adolescents, until the 1990s. Although it has recently leveled off, the trend in drug use steadily climbed upward for most of the past 15 years.

In the United States, the Office of National Drug Control Policy showed an alarming upward trend from 1991 to 2002. In that period, the rate of illicit drug use among Grade 8 students rose from 11 to 18 percent, and among Grade 12 students the rate rose from 30 to 41 percent. In Canada, the Ontario Student Drug Use Survey found that more than half of students surveyed in 2003 felt that drug use was higher than it had been in several years, and almost 30 percent felt that it was a "big problem" in their school. Use of cannabis alone doubled between 1989 and 2003.

Alcohol-use figures for young people are of even more concern. In 1997, the National Institute on Alcohol Abuse and Alcoholism reported that 26 percent of Grade 8 students and 51 percent of Grade 12 students drank alcohol within the previous month. The Parents Resource Institute for Drug Education showed in 2000 that 40 percent of junior high school students and 68 percent of senior high students consumed alcohol during the previous year. The Ontario Student Drug Use Survey showed similar figures: 39 percent of Grade 7 students consumed alcohol, as did 80 percent of students in Grades 11 and 12.

Of even more concern were the Ontario survey's figures for binge drinking, defined as having five or more drinks on the same occasion within the past month. About 1 in 10 students reported binge drinking two to three times during the month before the survey, and 45 percent of Grade 12 students had engaged in this kind of heavy drinking during the past year. These figures should be of great concern to all parents. Parents need to understand that teenage drinking is a problem and not to ignore its prevalence.

### Drugs, Alcohol, and Cigarettes

Despite the fact that federal spending on the drug war increased from $1.7 billion in 1982 to $17.7 billion in 1999, more than half of the students in the United States in 1999 tried an illegal drug before they graduated from high school. By Grade 12, 65 percent had tried cigarettes, and 35 percent smoked regularly. And, 62 percent of Grade 12 students and 25 percent of Grade 8 students in 1999 reported having been drunk at least once.

U.S. Office of National Drug Control Policy

Most of the surveys, in both the U.S. and Canada, indicate that drug and alcohol use among young people has reached a plateau. In some ways this is good news. As in the early 1980s, drug and alcohol education may be having an effect. Still, these figures are far too high for parents and educators to accept.

For many teenagers, the use of drugs is a risk behavior that is common to the age group. But many other teenagers report that they are using drugs for their temporary calming effect. For a short time, cares and concerns float away and they feel better. Reducing adolescent stress levels is a far healthier way to help our kids feel calmer and better about themselves.

## Tobacco Use

Recent studies vary slightly on the incidence of smoking among teenagers, but all are alarmingly high. In 2002 the U.S. Centers for Disease Control released its National Youth Tobacco Survey and pegged the number of adolescent smokers at 23 percent. A similar result was obtained by the Ontario Student Drug Use Survey, which showed that about 20 percent of the overall student population smoked. More alarming were the figures for Grade 12 students, which indicated that 30 percent were smokers. In Britain, a 2000 survey showed that 12 percent of English girls aged 11 to 15 years were regular smokers, compared with 9 percent of boys.

Of major concern in these figures are the consistent results that show that more girls are smoking than boys. Like the drug and alcohol figures, tobacco statistics have shown a recent decline as governments and educators have finally reacted to a trend that has been growing since the early 1980s. Nevertheless, the habit persists in high numbers. The worst aspect of this trend is that most adolescent smokers are addicted to nicotine and report that they want to quit but are unable to do so. About 95 percent of high school seniors who smoke think that they will not be smoking in five years, yet 75 percent of them become long-term smokers. The long-term health effects of this trend are well known and of great concern, yet smoking among adolescents continues at these high levels.

The effectiveness of the tobacco advertisers partly accounts for these very high smoking figures in the adolescent population. In the U.S., smoking advertisements in various media are still allowed, and some experts feel that the industry has been successful in convincing adolescents that this habit is the norm among their peers. In Canada, the only advertising that has been allowed in recent years is at sporting events (such as ski and car races), which have relatively limited exposure.

Another explanation for the high number of teenagers who smoke may be the ability of nicotine to temporarily alleviate their stress. The calming effect of this drug is well known. A major research effort of the National Household Survey on Drug Abuse in 2000 showed that school aspirations and performance played a major role in which students smoked. Those with lower performance, yet with high future goals, tended to smoke more. This appears to indicate that these students worried more about their marks and may be using cigarettes to help reduce their stress, at least on a short-term basis. If this is the case, it is most likely true that adolescents are relying on nicotine to reduce the effect of the many other stressors in their lives.

> **The British Response**
>
> The British Government in their 1998 White Paper "Smoking Kills," made reducing smoking among young people a priority. They allocated £100 million for an anti-smoking campaign over three years, including £60 million to build National Health services to help smokers quit and £50 million for a mass media education campaign.

## Obesity

A person is considered obese if he or she has 20 percent (or more) extra body fat for his/her age, height, sex, and bone structure. Using this measure, a Duke University study in 2003 found that the obesity rate among American children between 12 and 19 rose from 6 to 16 percent from 1974 to 2003. Poor diets and lack of exercise are considered to be the main causes of this disturbing trend. However, a further cause has recently been identified by Dr. Mary Dallman. She suggests that high-fat and high-carbohydrate foods inhibit the release of stress hormones. People suffering from chronic stress may have a constant urge to eat these foods because they end up feeling less tense and anxious. Dr. Dallman suggests that "people eat comfort food in an attempt to reduce the activity in the chronic stress-response network with its attendant anxiety."

**Obesity in North American Youth**

A comprehensive study released by the World Health Organization, entitled "Health Behaviour in School-aged Children," shows that 15-year-olds in the U.S. lead all of the 35 countries surveyed in obesity. Canadian teens of the same age ranked fourth. These are frightening results from countries that are considered to be leading the world in so many more positive areas.

Teenagers feeling constant stress may eat high-fat foods to reduce their anxiety. The result is that they gain weight, often to the obese level, which then produces more stress, as body image is a major concern for today's adolescents. A vicious cycle then emerges—eating to feel better, then feeling worse about gaining weight, then eating more to reduce the new stress.

## High Blood Pressure

Until very recently, blood pressure was rarely measured in children and adolescents because no one saw it as a problem. As a result, we have little information about what affects their blood pressure and whether it has changed from one generation to the next. One study conducted between 1988 and 2000 showed that children's systolic blood pressure was 1.4 mm Hg higher in 2000 than in 1988 and their diastolic pressure was 3.3 mm Hg higher. Both readings are very statistically significant and indicate an unwelcome change upward in the blood pressure of children between the ages of 8 to 17. The authors of the study attribute these rising blood pressure levels partly to the increase in obesity in children and teenagers. But they were unable to account for the majority of this increase. Stress is known to increase blood pressure in adults, and it is entirely possible that much of the blood pressure increases among our youth are the result of increased stress in their lives. Much research has yet to be done, but this is a very worrying trend as the health implications are dire for these young people when they become adults.

## Why Our Kids are Stressed

The levels of anger and violence, depression, obesity, and drug, alcohol, and tobacco use among our young people are clear indicators that their stress levels are far too high. The causes of this stress must be identified and solutions found in order to reverse these negative trends.

Where did all this stress come from? Why are children and youth turning to so many unhealthy and even dangerous behaviors? There has been a dramatic shift in attitudes and values in our society, a shift that has been disastrous for children. Though the changes have occurred in all parts of society, they are not unrelated. Rather, they have emerged like a cascading waterfall, one flowing out of another, tumbling down on the heads of children.

Social movements such as the women's movement restructured family life, as women headed into the workplace in greater numbers. For many men and women, paid work has taken on far greater value in their lives, and family life and parenting have become less important. With this greater emphasis on work has come affluence, which has given us more money than any generation before and has left many families with misplaced priorities.

As society has placed a premium on work rather than on parenting, social values once considered "sacred," such as marriage and raising one's own children, have given way to divorce and daycare. Parents no longer see education as a way to instill values in their children, but as a way to make sure their children "get ahead." Discipline, too, has fallen by the wayside, discarded by parents who are too afraid to rein in their children. And without proper guidance from parents, children become confused, with dangerous results: aggression, violence, obesity, anorexia, and the use of drugs, alcohol, and tobacco.

While many social factors are at play, they all contain a common thread: the role (or absence) of parental guidance. This is the parenting crisis, a situation where parents have lost their ability and even their willingness to become involved in the lives of their children, to communicate with them, to be active parents. The sad part is that it is not the parents who suffer the most, but the children.

# CHAPTER II
# Value Shifts

F ew would argue that the more importance parents place on their family, the more comfortable children are in that family and the less stress they feel both in the home and outside it. Unfortunately, the importance of the family has slipped for many parents over the past generation. This has not been a conscious decision process, but other values have emerged to interfere with the importance of raising children. The two that most concern our discussion are the growth of the women's movement and the renewed importance of the work ethic with its by-product, affluence. For women, these values often overlap, but the influence of these two values on both sexes is having a highly negative impact on child raising.

## The Impact of the Women's Movement

We will begin with perhaps our most controversial argument: that feminism and the women's movement contributed to a parenting crisis and the rise in children's stress. Before making our case, we must be clear: there is no doubt that the women's rights movement was necessary and that the reforms created by this movement were all too slow in coming. The fact that women are graduating from universities and graduate schools at rates well above that of men, and that almost all careers are now open to women, is testament to the transformation of our society.

What is controversial is our position that by emphasizing the value of women's rights and striving to achieve equality with men, women have put themselves into a conflicted position when it comes to child raising. To be equal with men, particularly in the career world, women must take themselves out of the home for long hours and subject themselves to the stresses and strains of the wage-earning world. This not only shortens the time available to spend with their children, but also creates more tired, stressed mothers when they arrive home. It has also created tremendous guilt for working mothers who recognize that they too have a right to fulfill themselves intellectually and socially by having a career, but who also wonder if they are not shortchanging their children by doing so. At the same time, the expected role of fathers has changed only slightly. Even now, few men consider staying at home with the children to replace working mothers. Instead, a new child-raising philosophy has emerged that questions why anyone should have to stay at home for any length of time to raise the kids. And in many circles, this philosophy goes so far as to refuse to even question whether having someone else raise the children is in fact superior to the parents doing it themselves. This is a major shift in values and its impact on families cannot be ignored.

## The Dilemma

For many women who came of age in the second half of the twentieth century, wider career choices offered work beyond that of wife and mother, and the traditional jobs in nursing, secretarial pools, and teaching. According to changing theory, only through the career world could a woman liberate herself from these stereotypical positions and find true self-expression and fulfillment. It is little wonder that many women were bored and angry about their fixed status in life and, the women's movement has worked hard to open up new opportunities for women accordingly.

From a child-raising viewpoint, however, such opportunities have a downside. The facts of biology mean that women must bear the children and breastfeed them through their early development (although even the need for the latter has been called into question). This forms a bond of trust between the two, which is a key factor in the development of stable and emotionally healthy children. The bonding process, and its close relation attachment, will be examined in more detail in the next chapter, but suffice it to say here that if it does not develop in a normal, healthy fashion, then the results can be very negative for the children and for family relationships.

The development of close bonding between mother and child can be impaired, for example, if the mother does not stay home with the baby, at least for the first year of its development. Further attachment problems can develop after that if one of the parents is not at home prior to the child starting school. In earlier generations, mothers were expected to stay home to raise their children, and most who could afford to do so did. But recently, many women have abandoned the traditional role for the new corporate image, so that someone else must raise their children. This brings with it the essential parenting dilemma.

The dilemma is that while embracing corporate life, most women experience at least some guilt about leaving their children for others to raise. They deeply love their children, but also want to find personal fulfillment in paid work. As a result, many women are unsure whether by working outside the home, they are doing the right thing for their children. Meanwhile, wage-earning women also must deal with social pressures. Well known as an influence on teenagers, peer pressure also influences women to remain in the work force, or to return swiftly after having a child. Several young professionals interviewed by the author described the power of this peer pressure and sought assurance that they were doing the right thing by returning to work. This dilemma constantly sits in the back of young mothers' minds and adds to the stress already created by the demands of working full-time and then being a part-time parent.

## Has the Pendulum Swung Too Far?

The dilemma described above is an indicator that perhaps the pendulum of change has swung too far. It seems that in addressing the many inequalities that existed between men and women, the women's movement reshaped women's values in a way that failed to take into account not only their strong maternal instincts, but also the needs of young children.

The role of wife and mother has been devalued to the point that anyone choosing to stay home with the kids is often subjected to derision and ridicule from their friends and colleagues. Why would anyone subject themselves to such endless drudgery and unstimulating isolation, the critics exclaim, when they could be using their intelligence, creativity, and leadership in the (paid) working world? Many critics disparage mothers who choose to stay at home and raise their children by comparing them to famous television wives such as Margaret Anderson on *Father Knows Best*, June Cleaver on *Leave It to Beaver*, or Harriet Nelson from *Ozzie and Harriet*, women considered to be the attractive servants of their husbands.

A closer look at these shows, however, reveals a very different picture. Instead of mindless tools of their male masters, all three of these women stood at the emotional center of the family. They provided a voice of reason when the other family members, including dad, were succumbing to impulsive or emotional behavior. This would seem to be a critical role in any family, yet it has been completely depreciated by many critics.

To be sure, taking care of children does involve a number of routine, boring tasks that are often less "exciting" than the tasks of the "working" world. Yet we cannot lose sight of the short-term and long-term rewards: the close bonding and attachment between parent and child, the ability to transmit values and beliefs on a constant basis, and the opportunities to witness the magical moments of childhood—baby's first smile, first crawl, first steps, first words, and the endless joys of engaging in a child's development.

For the sake of the children and their relationship to their parents, then, the pendulum must swing back to allow for more effective child raising, without compromising the gains women have worked so hard to achieve. It must swing back to a place where children are highly valued and where parents—mothers *and* fathers both—accept that parenting is an extremely important role that contributes to the stability and happiness of their children.

## Swinging the Pendulum Back

For that pendulum to swing, parents must make some compromises and adjustments to their lifestyle. These compromises are not easy. The first one is economic. If both parents are working, major financial losses will be incurred when one decides to stay at home. Maternity benefits range from 0 to 16 weeks in the United States, while in Canada, mothers can receive a relatively generous 50 weeks of benefits, but only when the mother meets specific employment criteria. Yet none of the benefits provide full salary, if salary is provided at all, and neither do the benefits provide for the amount of time off that is necessary to meet the needs of the children. As a result, financial sacrifices must be made for the years that the children are at home. Parents can do this by such expedients as driving an older model car, buying a smaller house, perhaps well away from major suburbs, and having fewer "toys" such as big screen TVs and motorboats. In other words, the compromise involves lowering expectations for several years until the kids are in school. In this day and age this is difficult, as most people tend to have very high expectations as to what life should be like.

For economic reasons, many mothers with young children must work. There are no two ways about it. It's always been this way, and they have regularly done the absolute best for their children through often difficult times. Nevertheless, I maintain that children can and often suffer stress when their mothers are not at home. If it is possible that one parent not work, certain compromises should be made for the sake of the children.

Because of the importance of breastfeeding, it is the mother who needs to stay home for at least the first year of a young child's life. Breastfeeding is another topic that will be addressed in detail in the next chapter, but most parenting authorities consider it to be vital, both for the development of the maternal bond and for the physical health of the child. The recommended length of time varies from expert to expert but a year is generally considered to be a minimum. Once this phase is done, it matters less which parent stays home with the kids. If the mother has the potential to earn more, then perhaps she should be the breadwinner. Or, if she really feels unsuited to staying at home for a few years, then perhaps the dad could stay at home until the kids are in school. More and more men are choosing to stay at home with the children these days, and the old stigma associated with "house husbands" is slowly vanishing — especially now that many wives are making more than their husbands.

If one parent should stay home, then how should that parent deal with some of the boredom and drudgery of housework. While a young baby needs considerable care, especially when the child becomes ambulatory, there is still considerable time not completely filled. Rather than watching daytime TV, stay-at-home parents could take distance education courses to upgrade their professional standing while away from the paid workforce. They can also volunteer at libraries, or other institutions where they can take the child. Also if another child comes along during the at-home period, there will be very little down time and this problem virtually disappears.

The women's movement, after a very slow start, has made huge changes in our society, most for the greater good. Unfortunately, it has also helped create a situation where there is far more stress in families today because there is no parent at home during the day, especially during the first five years of a child's life. Instead of valuing child raising and the family, the women's movement has often focused on the individual, usually through success in a career. This has created tremendous stress for women, especially young mothers who want to stay home with the kids but feel that to do so would be to shortchange themselves. Added to this stress is the peer pressure from those who have accepted these career-first values and feel that anyone who doesn't may be weakening the women's movement. Changes must be made so women can feel satisfied in the fact that raising emotionally stable children is also an important, and essential value. Women should also feel free to make the changes in their lives that are necessary to allow this to happen.

This is starting to happen. Newspaper stories are frequently appearing that describe young mothers who choose parenthood over careers. Unfortunately, this is still far too infrequent. Only the strongest and most financially stable women can make this break from mainstream thinking. If this trend continues and if husbands join in by taking their turn staying home with the kids, then perhaps the family will again become an important value.

## The New Work Ethic

Standing in the way of a pendulum shift back to child-centered parenting is a modern work ethic. Not since the early days of Protestantism, as espoused by John Calvin in the 1500s, has work been valued so highly as at the beginning of the 21st century. This is a fascinating development, because as recently as the 1960s and 1970s, social theorists were predicting the end of the 40-hour workweek and the imminent arrival of the 4-day week. Fascinating prognostications were made about what people would do with all their spare leisure time. Today, these dreams of expanded leisure no longer exist. Instead, society has reversed directions, with work now seen as a way to find individual meaning and to define oneself. Being a "success" is now defined in terms of achievement at work, and although this often brings with it wealth and affluence, it is the achievement that is most important. Somehow modern society has radically changed its focus, from its emphasis on family and dreams of leisure-time activities, to stressing the importance of being a good worker. This renewed value is a major culprit in downgrading the family as a major value. By substituting long hours and high stress levels, parents have much less time for their families and much less patience during the leisure time that they do have. How did this scenario—unthinkable just a generation ago—unfold? Let's consider a few recent trends.

## The Rise of the New Work Ethic

The renewal of the Protestant work ethic is a relatively recent phenomenon that appears to have its roots in the early 1990s when a combination of factors arrived together to cause working people to view their jobs differently.

The first of these circumstances was the general recession in 1990-91. As a result of these severe economic times, companies downsized, merged, right-sized, and restructured to become more efficient or "streamlined." Even after the recession ended, companies remained fearful that the economy could turn against them again and stayed conservative in their hiring policies. For example, the United States Department of Labor reported that about 8.3 percent of workers lost their jobs between 1990 and 1991. But from 1993 to 1995, when the economy had already emerged from its slump, another 7.2 percent of the work force was eliminated. In other words, almost as many people lost their jobs after the recession as they had during it. Companies continued to eliminate entire departments and "outsourced" many of their needs. The result was that many people became insecure about their jobs; they had to increase their work hours and productivity to remain employed.

Another major factor in the revival of the work ethic has been the role technology has played in the workplace. Once touted as a potential labor saver, the computer and other technological gizmos have actually increased workloads throughout the professional world. Both the laptop computer and the cellular telephone have extended the workplace outside of the office walls — to the airplane (business traveler working on a presentation during a long flight), and the home (telecommuter connecting to the central office via a private computer network). Such improvements in technology have helped increase productivity, but have also managed to extend the workweek well beyond the traditional 40 hours.

In fact, in the professional world, huge increases in time spent on the job have been recorded. For example, an unpublished 2002 study by the United States Department of Labor found that those in administrative, managerial, and executive occupations spent on average 45 hours a week at work. This is undoubtedly an underestimate because it does not take into account time spent performing wage and salaried work from home. Also in 2002, the New York-based Families and Work Institute published its National Study of the Changing Workforce, which found that the proportion of married wage and salaried employees who form part of dual-earning couples, increased from 66 percent in 1977 to 78 percent in 2002. The combined work hours these dual-earner couples with children put in rose from 81 hours a week in 1977 to 91 hours in 2002. This is an amazing development, given how hard workers struggled over the years to achieve a 40-hour week, and how the predictions from a generation ago were for an even shorter week.

Finally, the renewed work ethic was also bolstered by the continued influx of women into the workforce. The addition of large numbers of qualified women to the labor market increased competition for jobs in fields where such competition was previously much more limited. This has been particularly true in the professional world including management, medicine and other health professions, law and the administrative levels of teaching.

It is clear from these figures that people are working longer and harder, yet few parents are happy about this development. However, this is not necessarily the case with younger workers. Those that have been entering the work force for the last decade have been faced with examples of their managers and administrators clearly engaged in this new work ethic. To these young employees extremely hard work is the way it should be and they have almost completely embraced this standard. It has become a value for them and they are accepting it as a vital part of their lives. Their work defines their identities; they are what they are paid to do. They feel that by making work the center of their world, they are doing the right thing—emphasizing the right value.

## What's Wrong with the New Work Ethic?

There are several problems created by placing the value of work over more traditional values like that of the family. The first is obvious—the children in existing families are being shortchanged. Parents simply cannot spend the time with their children that they could were they to work a standard 9-to-5 day. Even the time they do have is tainted by fatigue and stress. Lacking energy and patience means that simple, enjoyable family activities like playing board games, going bicycle riding, and even walking the dog together rarely happen. Yet it is precisely during these relaxed and enjoyable times that the sense of family really develops and open communication can take place.

> "The salaries for a lot of these jobs have stagnated. The expectations while you're working these long hours have gone up. It's putting a tremendous amount of pressure on family life."
>
> **Dr. Jerry Jacobs, University of Pennsylvania**

Researchers have recently highlighted the impact of not being home with the kids. A 1999 study by Luthar and Avanzo showed that one of the reasons for the high rates of adjustment disturbances and substance use among affluent suburban junior high school students was disconnection from adults. In other words, the fact that their parents were not at home to supervise, especially in the after-school time period, contributed to their alienation from their parents and the development of such adjustment problems as clinical depression and increased drug and alcohol use.

A second potentially negative result of this new work ethic is the fact that professional women are choosing not to have children, or are limiting the number of children they have (usually to one) because they do not believe that they can have children and successful careers at the same time. This trend was very recently illustrated in a study conducted by Carleton University in Ottawa entitled "Voices of Canadians: Seeking Work-Life Balance." Almost a third of women studied had no children at all, and an equal number had just one. The majority of the women interviewed stated that they had made a conscious decision on how many children to have and that their career was a major factor in the decision. The decision to postpone having children until careers are well established, while well intentioned, can backfire, however. Many women who choose to wait to have kids are finding it difficult to become pregnant. This appears to be associated with stress and fatigue rather than with any physiological problems. The pressures and lengths of the workdays often make sex more infrequent among career couples. Even when they do have intercourse, stress from the tensions of the day or perhaps from the fact that they realize their biological clock is ticking reduces the likelihood of conception. The association between stress and the inability to get pregnant is well known, as couples that have tried for years to conceive, and then adopt a child, often find themselves pregnant shortly thereafter.

The implications of either not having children or of having a very small family are huge. The major one is that those who put their careers ahead of family are unlikely to change these priorities after having children. This means that they will drop the kids off at daycare as soon as possible after birth, and then continue to put in the same number of hours of work as before. To be sure, this is not always the case, as sometimes the effect of having children is electric on the parents and they decide to make lifestyle changes accordingly. For most parents who embrace the new work ethic, however, the presence of children will likely be a minor speedbump in their careers, not a major roadblock.

## Affluence

While the negative implications of the new work ethic mentioned above can be extremely serious, the affluence that the work ethic produces is equally problematic.

There is little doubt that the present generation has more disposable income than any generation of the past. The problem is that once a relatively high standard of living has been obtained, it fuels a desire for even more. While work is now seen as a value in itself, in that it defines who the person is and is seen to make the person worthwhile, its byproduct, affluence, is also becoming more highly valued. The things that people can buy also helps define them, so that the more they have, the better a person they feel they can become. Younger families are buying into this value belief shift quite literally — with the feeling that to be successful they need big houses, multiple cars, and any other trappings of success that they can acquire.

In 1960, the average house size in North America was 1100 square feet. Today, the average North American house size is 2350 square feet. In 1960, that average house cost $16,500 when wages averaged about $4,500 per year. The relative monster house of today, according to the U.S. Federal Housing Finance Board, costs $235,700, on an average salary of about $36,500. The ratio differences are obvious. In 1960 the average home was only 3.66 times the average yearly stipend; today, the average home costs 6.45 times the annual salary. One can see why in so many families both parents are working. Material affluence is expensive.

It is the same story with the other big-ticket household item, the car. Rarely are people content with a 5-year-old used vehicle as family transportation. Instead people seem to "need" an SUV as the primary vehicle, together with another relatively new car as back-up. Young people starting out rarely give thought to making do with an older vehicle. At an average starting sticker price of just over $30,000, new vehicles take several years to pay off. When the car loan is added to the mortgage payment, there is no doubt that both parents will need to work.

> **The SUV Story**
>
> SUVs average 33 percent less fuel efficiency than cars. The cost of owning an SUV is significantly more than the cost of owning even a mid-sized sedan. According to AAA Wisconsin, it cost $0.517/mile to drive a regular car in 2003. The average cost of operating an SUV in 2003 was $0.561/mile.

This story continues. Multiple TV sets and electronic gear, new furniture, and sparkling new appliances are needed inside the house. A refrigerator that does not dispense ice cubes, or does not have room enough for a banquet of food, is not acceptable. Eventually a vacation home can be added to the other payments, and the beat goes on. Little consideration is given to the idea of "making do" with what can be afforded.

There are alternatives to valuing affluence and material goods to the point where it is absolutely necessary that both parents work. These involve shifting one's perspective on what is really needed.

> • **Home.** The biggest step would be to find a house that can be afforded on one salary. This might involve moving to a satellite town rather than buying a new home in the local suburbs, or perhaps purchasing a "fixer-upper" that can be gradually improved as money becomes available. Or find work in a smaller, less expensive city.

> • **Car.** The next step would be to purchase only used vehicles that are fuel-efficient. A new car with a sticker price of $30,000 is less than half the price three years later.

Cars today last an average of 13 years. That means there are many good years left on the vehicle even when the price is down in the $10,000 range.

• **Household Furnishings.** Used household furnishings are readily available through "Bargain Finder" type newspapers and estate sales.

This whole process involves a very radical mind and value shift. It means putting family ahead of money and material things. It may even mean taking a lower paying or less prestigious job in a smaller community, possibly even in a different part of the country, just to locate an affordable home. The lower salary is made up quickly by the much lower cost of living. There is no need to live a subsistence lifestyle or take a massive drop in the standard of living. It just means buying a 1200-square-foot home instead of a 4000-square-foot monster and a three-year-old mid-size sedan instead of an SUV gas-guzzler. There will be lots of time for the toys once the kids leave home, which is only about 20 years away. If this sounds like a long time, look back at how fast the last 20 years have gone.

## Affluence and the Kids

The desire that our children have a better life than we did is a natural one in parents. For the most part, however, most parents of today do not have that bad a life. Raised in the 1970s and 1980s, the standard of living for most people was already relatively high. Despite this, parents today continue to try to enrich their children's material lives, even though there is no need for the kids to have more or better goods than did their parents. As one might guess, this creates problems for parents and children.

The relative high levels of affluence of today's parents give them the resources to make their kids lives very comfortable indeed. And they are proceeding to do just this. The money that they are making available to their children gives these kids the idea that cash is an unlimited resource. They want for nothing and this makes them want even more. Gone are the days, for example, of giving children a weekly allowance and too bad if they spend it all in one day. Instead parents hand out money whenever the children ask for it, teaching them nothing about budgeting, saving, or the value of a buck. Some parents have even reported that they do not believe in allowances because they do not believe their children should go without anything the parents can afford.

This is nonsense. The world does not work like that. In the real world money must be earned, and borrowed money must be paid back. Most people do not get what they want when they want it, and there is no reason for children to believe this is true. It merely makes them greedier and unappreciative.

A recent study by Columbia University's National Center on Addiction and Substance Abuse confirms what happens when children have too much money. Teenagers with $25 or more to spend were nearly twice as likely to have tried marijuana than kids with less available money. Admittedly, it was not found to matter whether the subjects in the study had obtained the money from their parents or from work, but that brings up another issue. Why are teenagers from relatively affluent homes working during the school year anyway? Isn't their main job school? While working in the summer can certainly be a good experience and teach several valuable lessons, there is no reason for teenagers to be working. The main reason offered by teens for working is to get money to buy things. The problem is that they don't need most of those things, especially drugs.

By allowing their children to work part-time during the school year, parents are passing on to their children the drive to acquire and the taste for affluence. They are also increasing the stress on these children by adding to their daily workload. Not only do these children now have to contend with the standard pressures of succeeding in school, but they now have to deal with the demands of working anywhere from 10 to 40 hours a week. The jobs they are able to obtain usually involve dealing directly with a demanding public, as in the fast-food industry, a stressor that most young people are ill-equipped to handle. They often also have to deal with demanding bosses, which for highly emotional teens, can be extremely difficult. Just committing these extra hours per week can be stressful as fatigue often leads directly to a shortening of tempers and increased frustration.

A good work ethic can be better taught by parents who help their children to become hard-working students. There is no need to allow them to enter the work force during the school year as this can increase their stress levels, possibly decrease their school performance, and teach them values that can often be inappropriate.

## The Tween Phenomenon

There is another problem stemming from the relation between affluence and kids, and this has to do with the "tween" phenomenon. This term describes kids in the 8- to 12-year-old age group who are acting in many ways like their older teenage siblings. It seems that major companies, seeking new and expanded markets, realized that children in this age bracket had more money to spend than ever before and were therefore a legitimate advertising target. Clothing, music, computer games, and electronics are being marketed directly to these young children through glossy magazines and television advertisements. Now, pre-teenage youngsters have become aware of fashions and music that previously had only attracted older teenagers.

It is estimated that by 2005, 30 million tweens in the United States will be spending nearly $41 billion on consumer goods. Canadian estimates are somewhat more modest with 2.5 million tweens slotted to spend $1.7 billion of their own money annually. These tweens also influence the spending of the rest of their families, to the tune of $20 billion.

Media and advertisers drool at these numbers. The tween market segment has become so crucial to producers that special organizations have sprung up to teach marketers and promoters how to sell to this group of children. Here is a typical pitch from one of these organizations taken from an upcoming conference on the subject:

> They're 10 going on 16...not kids, not teens...they're Tweens. Viewing themselves as sophisticated and mature, they have an attitude that's all their own. Tweens have become one of the nation's most significant consumer groups. Huge amounts of music, television, games, electronics, fashion and food are being marketed in their direction and they're buying.

Many different segments of the media are involved in this marketing attack on youth, including such teen magazines as *Nickelodeon*, *Teen People*, *Sports Illustrated for Kids*, and *YM*, as well as television commercials. Music videos also have a significant influence on tween clothing and fashion trends.

Obviously, this phenomenon could not have happened had the amount of money available to these youngsters remained curtailed. Instead, parents have willingly opened the vaults to their children at younger and younger ages. The result? Children who are growing up too fast. More troubling is the fact that, in looking like teenagers, tweens are also starting to act like them. Let's look at some of the disturbing trends:

- **Drug and Alcohol Use.** The Center for Disease Control and Prevention, 2000, showed that between 6 and 10 percent of the population in the 11–12 year old group use drugs. In 1999, more than 32 percent of young people reported that they began drinking before age 13.

- **Sexual Activity.** Until recently, tween-age children were not expected to experience sexual arousal. While intercourse is still uncommon in pre-teens, a new trend

> ### The Youngest "Tween"
>
> Perhaps the youngest child I've encountered showing "tween" behavior was a six-year-old, who was brought to me for being strong-willed and difficult to deal with. She threw complete temper tantrums if she was not allowed to wear clothing her mother thought was too mature for her. This very young girl, just barely into Grade 1, was able to say to this therapist that she didn't like the clothes her mother chose for her – she wanted to wear what her friends were wearing. This included belly shirts and tight pants. Part of the difficulty was a disagreement between parents on how to handle this child's demands, but much of the conflict was the result of the influence that the media had already had on both her and her peers.

shows that sudden popularity in oral sex among tweens and teenagers alike. A 2002 study by Health Canada indicated that by the time children get to Grade 9, 1 in 3 students had participated in this activity.

• **Depression and Suicide.** Where once there was doubt that depression even existed in these youngsters, suicide is now the sixth leading cause of death among the 5 – 14 age group, and the rate has doubled in the past generation.

Although affluence alone does not create such problems, the "free money" that parents dispense to their children creates a sense of entitlement and heightened expectations among younger children that leads them to behave like their older siblings. Furthermore, parental attitudes toward money reflect wider parenting problems.

The first is the problem of "enabling parents." These are parents who actually encourage their youngsters to grow up faster than necessary. Kay Hymowitz, author of *Ready or Not: What Happens When We Treat Children as Small Adults*, says that "a surprising number of parents, far from seeking to undermine their children's tweenishness, are enablers of it." They do this in many ways. For example, to enhance their children's social life and make them popular with their peer group, they ensure that the kids have all the right clothes, plenty of money, and even help them to throw stylish parties. Parents of children from one western Canadian private school pointed angrily to a set of parents who even provided liquor for their tween to dispense at his parties.

Enabling parents also may push their children to succeed in the entertainment, sports, or academic fields. The motivation for these parents may be as simple as wanting more for their children than they had, or it may be much more complicated. In *The Hurried Child*, David Elkind wondered if parents who pushed their children to grow up too soon weren't doing so out of some problem related to their own job dissatisfaction, or to relieve their personal frustrations. This type of parent may be using their "trophy" children to improve their own status in society.

"Absentee parents" also contribute to tweenishness. These are parents who are working long hours and whose children are in school. If the kids are not involved in extracurricular activities, they often arrive home before 4:00 p.m., and have to entertain themselves until their parents arrive from work. Lacking adult behavioral models, these "latchkey kids" look to their peer group for influence. Where once they relied on their parents to buy their clothes and control any desires to indulge in the fads and fashions of the older teenage kids, they fall back by default on their friends and acquaintances. The result is imitation of the age group they most admire—the apparently carefree and independent adolescents.

Finally, tweens can flourish in an environment of "passive parenting." Many modern parents are confused about how to discipline their children and what they should be passing on to their kids about the most effective ways to act in society. They feel that they will be damaging their children's self-esteem if they apply consequences for misbehavior. The combination of this confusion with the lack of time and energy created when both parents work long hours, is resulting in children having to find their own set of morals and values. Again, in the absence of a responsible adult model, tweens follow the examples presented to them in the media and by their friends. When parents fail to apply consequences for illegal or immoral behavior on the part of their young children, the kids become confused as to what is right and wrong. This is then compounded when the parents do not take the time to communicate their moral values on such issues as sex and alcohol and drug use.

These parenting issues are far more important to the development of the tween phenomenon than is the influence of the media. While the media and advertising industry certainly contributed to the problem, parents can counteract this influence by controlling their children's money supply, teaching them their morals and values, restricting the content of what they watch, and disciplining them if their behavior is counter to these morals and values. If parents cannot influence the behavior of their 8- to 12-year-olds, they will certainly not be able to influence their teenagers.

And one of the best places to begin exerting that influence is in the pocketbook. No matter how wealthy the parents, there are solid reasons for not sharing this wealth too soon. To learn the value of money, children should have a limited amount, such as a weekly allowance, then be taught how to save for desired items. Giving them what they want, all the time, teaches them the wrong lesson about life and encourages them to grow up far too fast.

The shift toward parent-centered values and away from parenting-centered values has diminished the importance of hands-on parenting. The women's movement, for all its successes and contributions, has had a negative impact on mothering, and the new work ethic has reduced families to secondary status. Parents might be giving their children more things, but they are not giving their children what really matters: their time and attention. In fact, as the following chapter makes clear, the social pressures to let other people raise one's children are so strong that it becomes difficult to transmit one's own values.

# CHAPTER III

# The Daycare Debate

**T**he relative merits of daycare is one of the most taboo topics of discussion among modern parents. Daycare is a "sacred cow" not to be attacked or criticized. Many parents do not want to hear anything negative about daycare, because it might mean that they have to rethink their economic standards and goals. Instead there continues to be a huge demand, both in North America and Europe, for governments to provide more daycare at lower costs. In fact, in its 2004 election campaign the Liberal Party of Canada promised $7.5 billion over 5 years for various caregiver programs, and indeed came up with $5 billion in its subsequent 2005 budget. The opposition, the Conservative Party, promised only to increase the amount parents were allowed to deduct on their taxes for caregiver services. Neither party dared mention that there might be negative effects to placing young children in daycare. They were simply responding to what the voters were demanding. Similar demands are being heard in the U.S., in the European Community, and in Australia and New Zealand. In Norway, Sweden, and Denmark, these services are already provided to parents at relatively low costs, and Denmark even legislated that it is the right of the child to attend daycare and that institutions must be educational as well as provide possibilities for socialization.

Amazingly, despite daycare centers only being in existence in large numbers for about two decades, there is almost no debate about whether or not children should be in the centers, but only about how much daycare should be provided by governments. In fact, there has rarely been much debate over the relative benefits and concerns of placing young children in daycare. What social forces moved so quickly to virtually stifle any opposition to parents allowing strangers to parent their children?

## The Thrust for Daycare

There seems little doubt that the primary thrust for universal, affordable daycare originally came from the women's movement of the 1960s. The new woman, portrayed by the likes of Betty Friedan and Helen Gurley Brown, could do it all. Immediately after they had their babies, if they had them at all, they needed to go back to work so that they could achieve the fulfillment that a meaningful occupation provided, while achieving economic equality at the same time. To do this, someone had to look after the babies, and not everyone could drop them off at Mom and Dad's or find a nice lady to be the surrogate parent. The result was the push for organized daycare centers. Since this was considered to be the right and proper thing to do, no one wanted to question whether this was good for the child. Women really wanted to believe in the correctness of this lifestyle, as they

"In his pernicious action, Judge Carswell not only flaunted the Civil Rights Act, designed to end the job discrimination which denied women, along with other minority groups, equal opportunity in employment, but specifically defied the policy of this administration to encourage women in poverty, who have children, to work by **expanding daycare centers**, rather than having them depend on the current medieval welfare system which perpetuates the cycle of poverty from generation to generation."

**Betty Friedan, 1970, Testimony Before The Senate Judicial Committee in the Ida Phillip's case**

felt they couldn't possibly do it any other way, so daycare was an obvious solution.

Men also had a role in the veneration of daycare, if only a passive one. By either doing nothing to counter the feminist push for daycare, or by actively supporting it out of fear that to do otherwise was to deny women their rightful destinies, they aided and abetted the daycare movement. Men too failed to question whether being cared for by strangers was good for children, and instead cheerfully supported the assumption that it must be. They even were instrumental in implementing the affirmative action programs, also called reverse discrimination, which helped women get priority in getting jobs, making even more daycare necessary. Voices that did ask any questions were loudly drowned out, because if the question was to be asked, then people might not have liked the answer.

Hand in hand with the feminist promotion of daycare were the media. They tended to idealize the new woman as someone who could have it all—family and career combined, with no negative effects on anyone. It made good press as it was a message many women really wanted to hear. With this cheerleading ringing in their ears, these mothers actually believed that they could do it all, and the press and magazines willingly supported this notion.

Initially, no research data existed to counter these beliefs. The daycare movement was too young for any long-term studies of its effects on children. Researchers often need at least 20 years of longitudinal data for such life-course studies, and before this data could be gathered, it had become an accepted "fact" that children benefited from the socialization and extra learning that occurred in daycare settings. As Kay Hymowitz wrote in *Liberation's Children*, daycare advocates have always had the problem of having to reassure people that the long hours away from their children cause no harm. Hymowitz feels that this has been a very easy sell until recently because early studies showed no negative relations between daycare, infants' trust in their mothers, or language skills in daycare infants. Any previous research showing potential problems was either ambiguous or was hidden away.

Penelope Leach, the best-selling British parenting author and a more scientific successor to Dr. Spock, was even more blunt on this topic. Writing in *Children First*, Leach stated that Western media have played a substantial part in convincing people that not only does everyone go out to work these days, but everyone should. Leach feels that the media have glamorized the career woman as a supermom who can do everything all at once. Unfortunately, Leach argues, the media have not examined who is actually looking after the kids while these supermoms outsmart their male counterparts in the boardroom.

The message is clear that the media have been willing accomplices of those who insist that mothers can be all things to all people with no adverse affects on anyone. Leach and Hymowitz also argue that the figures given by the media and pro-daycare advocates exaggerate the high percentage of families needing daycare by lumping categories together and including women in the work force who do not actually require daycare.

To their credit, the feminists and media who promoted their ideas did so with a clear conscience. They really did believe what they were saying. Recently, however, a more sinister influence in the promotion of daycare has been identified. Brian C. Robertson, writing in *Day Care Deception: What the Child Care Establishment Isn't Telling Us* identifies a powerful daycare lobby that is promoting its services for financial gain. To this end they have attacked and distorted the findings of researchers that show that commercial daycare can harm young children emotionally, psychologically, and even physically. They have added their financial resources and media influence to promote daycare no matter if it cannot be shown to be good for children. Overall, Robertson makes a very convincing case against these daycare lobbyists and, in fact, against daycare itself.

### The Lobby Attacks the Author

As a result of an interview given to the local newspaper, the author was attacked for his views by the editor of an American women's literature magazine. Billed as "The Magazine for Thinking Mothers", *Brain, Child* is a "quarterly print publication that reflects modern motherhood the way it really is." This editor, Stephanie Wilkinson, wrote an editorial in which she stated the following:

> And what were Dr. Wooding's suggestions for fixing this crisis, anyway? On the problem of too much advice, I guess he's saying: don't listen to them; listen to me. As for divorce—just don't. And those selfish parents? They've just got to get over themselves and realize that they should stay at home for the first five years of each child's life. (That's when it struck me that Wooding isn't really talking about parents being selfish—he's talking about mothers. I doubt he's taking Dad to task for seeking fulfillment outside the home.)

The editorial went on to "prove" I was wrong. Frankly I was flattered that a journalist with a doctorate in European and American Religious History would take the time to slam me for my parenting views. Never mind that she never actually talked to me to see if these really were my views or if I had been quoted correctly. Never mind that she has no background in parenting and that her magazine features literature, not parenting expertise. It is a clear example of the sensitivity of the pro-daycare, pro-working mother lobby that for so long has attempted to stifle its critics.

In short, feminists, media, and the daycare lobby have combined to shout down anyone who questions whether it is actually good for children. For years it has been politically incorrect to even hint that mothers should stay at home to look after their children. In fact the barrage against mothers staying at home continues even today (see insert above) from all three sources. It takes courage to stand up to these sources and to publicize negative daycare research, and fortunately, some of these researchers are now coming forward.

## What Does Modern Research Show?

Over the past few years, researchers have begun to publish their studies of the effects of daycare. Many of these have begun to challenge commonly held assumptions about daycare. For example, it has long been accepted that "quality" daycare, generally defined as institutions with well-trained personnel and a low child/caregiver ratio will negate any harmful effects. Although this makes good sense logically, there is virtually no research evidence to support this reasoning, and in 2001, the National Institute on Child Health and Human Development in the United States found that children who spend the majority of their time in daycare are three times as likely to exhibit behavioral problems in kindergarten as those who were cared for primarily be their mothers. According to Dr. Jay Belsky, one of the study's investigators, children who spend more than 30 hours a week in childcare "are more demanding, more non-compliant, and they are more aggressive." These children displayed a greater tendency to get into fights, act cruel and mean, and bully. The study also found that, contrary to the accepted doctrine, time spent in childcare was linked more strongly with children's behavior than was the quality of the care.

Behavioural concerns were also at the core of a British government-funded research project. This research showed that "children who spent long hours in daycare before the age of 2 (especially in day nurseries and local authority centers) were more likely to have anti-social behavior at age 3."

The weight of this research led Dr. Belsky, formerly of Pennsylvania State University and now a professor of Psychology at Birkbeck College in London, to write that "whereas more time in childcare prior to starting school predicts higher levels of aggression and disobedience, less time spent in care predicts lower levels of such behavior." More to the point, "the adverse effects of lots of time spent in childcare emerged even when children were in high quality programs."

Rather than focus on behavior, a study by the Institute of Child Development of the University of Minnesota looked at the physiological responses of young children (younger than age 3) in full-day daycare. This study found that levels of cortisol, a key hormone in the stress response, increased during the afternoon on those days spent in daycare, but fell in the afternoons of days spent at home. Furthermore, cortisol levels were the highest and rose most steeply among those children judged by the daycare personnel as being the shyest. This finding led the study's lead author, Dr. Megan Gunnar, to argue that such shy children "struggle in group situations and find them stressful."

Finally, other research has looked at the educational outcomes of children in daycare. In Britain, a 2001 study for the Joseph Rowntree Foundation found that children of full-time working mothers are more likely to perform badly at school. Specifically, the study of 1200 young children determined that where a mother of pre-school children worked full-time for a year longer than the average 18 months, there was a fall of 12 percent in the likelihood of that child passing his or her A-level (the top academic level) exams. Even among children with mothers working part-time there was a 6 percent decrease in the chance that the child would attain A-level standing.

### Daycare Statistics

According to information gathered by the Children's Defense Fund in Washington, D.C., an organization that advocates for quality, affordable childcare, only about 25 percent of children are cared for by their parents. The other three-quarters of all children are cared for as follows:

- 30 percent in childcare centers
- 15 percent with family childcare providers
- 5 percent with in-home caregivers (nannies)
- 25 percent with relatives

In 2003, researchers at the Institute for Social and Economic Research in Britain discovered that children of mothers who return to work full-time in the years before they start school have slower emotional development and score less well on reading and mathematics tests. This research also complemented that of the Rowntree Foundation by showing that the child's chances of reaching A-level status dropped from 60 percent to 50 percent if the mother returned to work early.

The findings of all of these recent studies should be enough to give even the staunchest daycare advocates cause for concern about the possible negative effects that daycare is having on children. Unfortunately this is not always the case.

## The Research Controversy

Despite the number of studies indicating the dangers of daycare for young children, few researchers have been willing to take a strong stand against it. There are several possible reasons for this. The first is the difficulty of controlling variables in studies of young children. For example, if researchers wanted to examine whether daycare is a cause of children's disobediance, they have to "control" for other factors, or make sure that nothing else is contributing to this conduct. Unfortunately it is usually extremely difficult for the researchers to control for other variables such as parental disciplining methods, intelligence of the children, single-parent families, and hereditary emotional conditions such as ADHD or bipolar disorder. Experienced researchers always qualify their findings because they cannot find samples of children with exactly the same backgrounds and parents. This is obviously a legitimate concern.

It is one thing to qualifying one's findings, but something else to minimize the findings entirely, and this is what many researchers end up doing. This goes well beyond legitimate research concerns and seems to be more a defensive response to the criticism that researchers know will be forthcoming from daycare advocates.

Consider the experience with a study published in 2002 in the journal *Child Development*. This study found that daycare had "negative effects" on children's cognitive skills when the mothers worked 30 hours or more a week, "even when controlling for childcare quality, the quality of the home environment and maternal sensitivity." This research actually seems to have controlled more variables than most studies as it ruled out differences in the quality of the childcare, home environment, and the quality of the mothering.

Nevertheless, when reporters from the *New York Times* asked about the implications of this study (July 17, 2002) the authors began to backpedal immediately. Instead of pointing out the legitimacy of their findings, the authors emphasized that "the study shouldn't necessarily discourage mothers of young children from working, but encourage government policy that would improve the quality of childcare, change the length of family leave and include pay for those who take it, as well as promote job-sharing and flexible hours that would help working parents who struggle with work and caring for young children."

While there are several good suggestions contained in this summary, how can they possibly even suggest that the study should not discourage mothers from working? The results clearly show that mothers should indeed be discouraged. They even go so far as to suggest that governments should improve the quality of daycare when they had already concluded that childcare quality was not a factor in their results!

A similar result occurred with the National Institute of Child Health and Human Development (NICHD) study mentioned earlier. One of the researchers, Dr. Helen McCartney, "clarified" the results of this study in a 2001 issue of *Massachusetts Psychologist*. While admitting that the reported figures were correct, she stated, "The results are real but I think that there is a more nuanced version of the findings than was presented." What does that mean? The entire article was a clear attempt to mitigate the findings so that daycare advocates would not be upset and yet not once were the actual findings contradicted.

Dr. Jay Belsky knows well the perils of being anti-daycare. As early as 1986, he started suggesting that daycare might have detrimental effects on children. His comments about the same NICHD study, in which he was one of the researchers, drew stinging criticism from several of his colleagues, especially Dr. Sarah Friedman. Again without refuting the actual results of the study, she stated in the *New York Times* that "we have no way in this study to attribute cause and effect. In the case of these findings, there is no way to attribute causality" (April 26, 2003). This is researcher double-speak much like the "nuanced" comment above. Dr. Friedman is falling back on the difficulties of controlling variables rather than supporting her own research findings. She also criticized Belsky for identifying himself as the lead researcher, another red-herring that deflects attention away from the results themselves.

Brian C. Robertson, writing in *Daycare Deception*, feels that many researchers have their own anxieties to confront. He suggests that one of the main reasons for these researchers backing off from drawing negative conclusions about their own results is that they themselves are working mothers who put their own children into daycare. Robertson may have a point. It certainly seems very clear that no sooner are results negative to daycare announced, then the researchers start to explain them away. Certainly it is hard to draw clear conclusions from studies done on children, but the evidence is rapidly piling up and cannot all be explained away.

## Will Daycare Cause Children to be Serial Killers?

While it is all too common for researchers to minimize the results of their daycare studies, it is also possible to exaggerate in the opposite direction. No study has linked daycare to future criminal behavior of any kind, and this is unlikely to happen. Instead it seems clear that the negative effects of daycare are much subtler, while still of concern. Taking the results of studies that indicate that daycare can lead to behavior problems as an example, we could look at possible classroom effects once these children have entered school. If several of the daycare graduates exhibiting minor behavior problems are in the same class, the learning atmosphere could be seriously altered with the teacher having to spend more time in disciplinary and corrective activities. As the teacher expends time and energy managing the classroom, she will have less time and energy to teach and to introduce innovative activities. Continued year after year, the effects on the overall learning of each child could be significant. While most children could survive despite these challenges, albeit with a slower learning rate, those with learning difficulties, such as ADD or dyslexia, would be even more challenged in their attempts to learn.

Similar effects can be seen with children's ability to form intimate and trusting relationships. Poor experiences in daycare, or simply the lack of contact with their parents when they need it in their early years, could translate into difficulties forming relationships as adults. This means that the already high divorce rate, which has actually dropped in recent years, could remain at these high levels rather than continuing to decline. Obviously, parents cannot draw a direct connection between their child's divorce and their having been in daycare. Daycare might not be the only cause either, but if it contributes to the child's weakened ability to form relationships, then when combined with other circumstances, it might result in that child's bailing out of a relationship rather than working through the difficulties.

There is a lot of speculation here because the effects of daycare cannot be separated out from many other factors such as parental values, divorce, and poor disciplinary practices. Yet the research shows that daycare does have some effects and, no matter how subtle those effects are and no matter whether every child will show them, why would parents take the chance that their child could be effected? Parents must begin to pay more attention to the recent research and not try, as many of the researchers are, to whitewash the results.

## How About the Short Term Effects?

Suppose some brilliant researcher could show that there was no chance of any long-term effects of daycare on children. Would that make daycare acceptable? Not necessarily. There are many occasions when incidents occur that would normally be solved by comfort from a parent, but at daycare that comfort is not available. These incidents include such things as minor falls and bumps, frights from loud noises or sudden surprises, and fear of new situations as may occur on field trips. At these times children need their parents for immediate comfort. Instead they may or may not get any such comfort from the daycare staff. One could possibly argue that it makes the kids tougher and more adaptable, but really what is happening is that the kids are unhappier than they need be at this age.

A similar problem occurs with illness. How many children have to go to their caregiver when they are sick? Because it is so difficult for parents to take time off to be with their sick child, this tends to occur only with the most serious illnesses. The result is that kids have to be awakened in the morning and hauled off to the caregiver, just when they would be better off sleeping in and having their parent to administer to their needs when they awaken. The illness would likely heal faster, and the likelihood of passing it on to other children would be lessened. In fact, isn't it far more likely that a child will get sick in a daycare situation when surrounded by children with illnesses?

These are not huge problems perhaps, but they do make a child's life less enjoyable in the short term. Is this really necessary?

## What's Wrong With Our Daycare Centers?

But won't all these possible negative effects on childcare simply disappear if we have "quality" daycare centers (now often officially termed "childcare centers")? Such a question is constantly asked by parents, researchers, and the media. These quality centers would presumably be bright, airy, well-equipped facilities, staffed with well-trained, caring professionals, and have a low child/worker ratio and heavy involvement from well-informed parents. While this might be true in a perfect world, the reality is that, under present circumstances, such centers cannot exist. To create them would cost far too much money to make it worthwhile for both parents to work.

To begin with, most daycare centers today are in converted houses, church basements, or in surplus classrooms. Very few are in purpose-built buildings because the cost of building them would be prohibitive. This generally means that play facilities are limited and the quarters are often rather cramped. Most states and provinces regulate these facilities in terms of fire prevention and safety, and mandate a minimum space of only 35 to 40 square feet per child (and this measurement often counts the space in the entire building, not just in the childcare space). Air quality depends on the size of the building and number of children, but the majority lack upgraded ventilation systems, making sickness among the children more common. Generally, most facilities are smaller than they should be for their purpose.

Another factor inhibiting the development of "quality" daycare centers is the training level of the staff. According to a summary of Child Daycare Services provided by the United States Census Bureau, training requirements are most stringent for directors of childcare centers, less so for teachers, and minimal for childcare workers. This generally means that a director requires a college degree (although not always), teachers require a high school diploma and perhaps some college experience, and childcare workers *usually* need a high school diploma. In Canada, program supervisors or center supervisors are required only to have a 2-year college diploma in Early Childhood Education. Daycare workers in Alberta need only a 50-hour orientation course while those in Ontario need no courses at all!

In addition to having no standardized levels of training across jurisdictions, almost no states or provinces mandate what mix of directors, teachers, and workers is required in childcare centers of any size. Generally a director is required to open such a center and obtain a license from state, provincial, or local authority, but there is no apparent requirement to have any "teachers" on staff. Here, for example, are the Pennsylvania staffing requirements, which are typical of most states and provinces:

## Pennsylvania Child Care Ratios

| Age Group | Age Range | Ratio Provider to Child | Max in a Group | Ratio during Nap Periods |
|---|---|---|---|---|
| Infants | 0–12 months | 1 caregiver to every 4 children | 8 | 1 to 4 |
| Young Toddlers | 13–24 months | 1 caregiver to every 5 children | 10 | 1 to 5 |
| Older Toddlers | 25–36 months | 1 caregiver to every 6 children | 12 | 1 to 12 |
| Preschool | 37 months until1st day of 1st grade | 1 caregiver to every 10 children | 20 | 1 to 20 |
| Young School Age | 1st grade until 1st day of 4th grade | 1 caregiver to every 12 children | 24 | 1 to 24 |
| Older School Age | 4th grade until 15 years of age | 1 caregiver to every 15 children | 30 30 | 1 to 30 |

Note that only "caregivers," which require the least education or training, are specified. "Teachers" are apparently not required. This means that those caring for your children *could* have a high school diploma—but do not need to—putting them at little more than the babysitter level. This is clearly inadequate for working with groups of children on a daily basis who will have a wide variety of individual needs and problems.

Naturally, when educational requirements are low, salaries will also be minimal. This is precisely the case with childcare workers.

According to United States Bureau of Labor data from 2000, child-care workers earned on average $7.86 per hour. Preschool teachers, when they actually exist in childcare centers, earned a princely $9.66 per hour. That same year in Canada, childcare worker salaries averaged $22,717 per year, a level comparable to that of parking lot attendants. How committed to your children are workers receiving these kinds of salaries going to be?

Although there will certainly be some excellent childcare workers, even at these low salaries, other concerns arise as a result of this poor pay. Most of these positions require long hours, as centres must be open at least 12 hours a day to accommodate the various work hours of the parents. Traffic jams and unscheduled overtime often keep parents even later, and the centers cannot close until all children have been picked up. When these long hours are combined with the often-stressful working conditions, low pay, and lack of benefits, staff turnover tends to be quite high. In fact it is much higher than the average for all occupations. High turnover translates into little continuity of care for children in the majority of daycare centers, which can be very hard on the children, who will continually have to accustom themselves to different people and their differing philosophies and methods of caring.

The combination of low educational requirements with low salaries also means that childcare workers in licensed centers will usually have little understanding of effective disciplinary practices, individual differences, emotional disturbances, physical illnesses, or even expected behavior at the various ages. They will be reacting to the children on the basis of instinct and their own upbringing, which are hardly sufficient to meet the demands of large groups of children. Of course, at least in the licensed centers there are some standards. The majority of children, however, are in unlicensed facilities usually located in people's homes. While the numbers in such homecare settings are restricted (after a certain number of children, the caregiver must obtain a license),

**Daycare Turnover**

A report from the Center for the Child Care Workforce in Washington, D.C., titled "Worthy Work, Unlivable Wages," released in 1998 made the following observations:

• More than a quarter of childcare teachers (29 percent) and 39 percent of assistants left their jobs during the past year—an average turnover rate of 31 percent for all staff—at a time when the demand for their services has grown dramatically.

• One-fifth of centers reported losing half or more of their teaching staff during the past year.

• Only 14 percent of childcare teachers have remained on the job in the same center over the past decade, and only 32 percent have been employed in their centers for five years or more.

Independent non-profit centers are more likely to retain their teaching staff than are other types of programs, particularly those run by for-profit chains.

there are otherwise no standards at all. Unless the parents know this person intimately, the quality of the person raising their children will be in serious doubt.

Where, then, are these "quality" daycare centers that will magically improve the situation for children? The costs of childcare are already a major expense for those requiring this service. Childcare averages $35 a day ($700/month) in the Toronto area and can be over $1200 a month in other major centers such as New York or San Francisco. To offer quality service—with higher salaries, fuller staffing, and better facilities—childcare centers would have to double their fees. Most parents already have enough trouble paying for "non-quality" daycare, so it is highly misleading for experts and researchers to trumpet the beneficial effects of quality daycare. Except for a few experimental centers at universities, quality daycare does not, and likely will not, exist.

## The Effects of Maternal Deprivation

Beyond the negative effects on children, one crucial aspect of placing children in childcare that is rarely mentioned is the impact of removing a young child from its mother at an early age. The bond and attachment that forms between a mother and child, and later with the father as well, is considered to be a central factor in the later emotional stability of the child. Yet the impact of removing infants from their mothers for large parts of each day is rarely mentioned or discussed by the pro-daycare people.

Maternal deprivation first came to the fore in the late 1940s after studies by researchers such as Rene Spitz and Margaret Ribble. Later John Bowlby wrote at great length about the possible negative effects that this process might have on children. Unfortunately these early studies had serious design flaws, and some of the claims have since been shown to have been exaggerated. But despite those flaws, these early researchers had some very valid points that modern research has since confirmed.

> John Bowlby, writing in his classic *Child Care and the Growth of Love*, felt that an essential component of children's mental health is a warm, intimate and continuous relationship with the mother. He argued that this close and rewarding relationship with the mother, varied by intimate relations with the father and siblings, was the very foundation of character and good mental health.

## Bonding and Attachment

The first step in forming the relationship between mother and child is bonding. This is considered to be the trust that develops between the infant and its caretaker, which is usually the mother. This bond develops through repeated completions of the cycle:

infant need ⇨ crying ⇨ parental action to meet the need ⇨ satisfaction ⇨ relaxation

This trust develops in phases. In the first few weeks, the infant will respond to anyone who comforts it. After a few weeks infants are able to discriminate between people, and can pick out their parents from others. They now respond differently to their parents, smiling and making sounds to those they recognize, crying when these people leave, and being comforted by the soothing of the parents. After six or seven months, this bond becomes an attachment as the infants now show signs of an affectionate and lasting relationship with the primary caretaker, usually the mother. Infants now seek contact with the mother and show signs of affection for her by wanting to crawl into her lap or be held in her arms. They also may cry when the mother leaves their presence.

Attachment to the father tends to develop later than to the mother because father-infant interaction is usually less frequent than that with the mother and also is of a different nature. Mothers generally feed, bathe, dress, cuddle, and talk to their infants. Fathers, on the other hand, tend to play with their infants more, while doing less of the child maintenance. This is especially true if the mother is breastfeeding. Penelope Leach, writing in her best-selling *Children First*, has an excellent description of the father's role in this attachment process. She says that while infants cannot have too much closeness with their mothers, they also need caregivers who can serve as substitutes when their mothers are not available. She feels that fathers fill this role nicely as their comings and goings, usually out to work, offer a "balancing discontinuity" or a recurring treat. His difference from the mother, in feel and smell, combined with his obvious caring, make him an important factor in the baby's life.

Most infants with caring and sensitive mothers and involved and caring fathers form a secure attachment with their parents. Because of this security, the desire to be close to them is balanced by an urge to explore the environment. The parents become a secure home base from which the child can venture out to discover its immediate world. Insecure attachments, however, can be formed both by parents who neglect or reject (or occasionally abuse) the child. Insecure attachment can also occur when the child is frequently sick or disabled in some way. In these cases, the infants may ignore their mothers when they are approached. They may be angry when

## A Case of Insecure Attachment

One of the first serious cases to be handed to the author as a young school psychologist involved an extremely angry 14-year-old boy. Ian was always in trouble in school and when the tension built up too high, he would go out into the woods with his shotgun and shoot round after round into the trees until the gun was too hot to hold. On discussing these problems with his parents, Ian's mother surprised me by stating "He never loved me – right from the start."

Realizing, even at this early stage of my career, that this was a highly unusual statement for a mother to make, I asked about his infancy. She related that his first year after birth was a horrible experience. Ian was born prematurely and his digestive system was not fully formed. As a result he was in agony after every feeding, usually regurgitating every-thing. Feeding times became a nightmare as, instead of the contact with the breast soothing him, he reacted violently each time his mother held him close. Both mother and child came to dread his feeding time. This continued even after the parents had switched to a bottle and his diges-tive system could accept food.

His mother did not associate the early feeding problems with the later apparent rejection of her, and the relationship between them remained poor, despite both parents trying their best with him. Eventually the anger he felt over this apparent lifetime rejection was too much for him to contain and began spilling over into the classroom and with his peers. Understanding the reasons behind his anger helped, but he eventually dropped out of school and joined the army, which gave him the discipline he needed along with an outlet for his anger and he became an excellent soldier.

the mother leaves, yet will reject the mother's efforts at contact when she returns. When picked up they often immediately writhe and wiggle to get down.

A secure attachment is extremely important to a child, and research has shown that securely attached children tend to be bet-ter at developing relationships with others; are more cooperative, enthusiastic and persistent; are better at solving problems and attaining full intellectual potential; are more compliant and con-trolled; and are more popular and playful. These are powerful argu-ments for parents who want to ensure that the attachment between them and their infants are as secure as possible.

# The Effects of Daycare on Infant Bonding and Attachment

Although you would not know it by reading the popular press and articles by daycare advocates, research has been done on the effects of daycare on infant attachment. In a 1989 article, Dr. Allison Clarke-Stewart reported that infants in full-time daycare were somewhat more likely to be classified as insecurely attached. The recent research by the National Institute of Child Health and Human Development discussed earlier concluded that daycare does not harm the attachment of *all* children to their parents. Some interesting exceptions, however, showed how combinations of factors can cause trouble. Among mothers judged less sensitive to their 15-month-old children, each of these factors was associated with insecure attachment: more hours of daycare, low-quality care, or many different care situations. In other words, daycare itself could not be shown to cause attachment problems, but when combined with other factors the risk definitely increased. Even more forcefully, Dr. Jay Belsky concluded that "children who had experienced extensive nonmaternal care evinced all the signs of neediness, assertiveness, and aggression, regardless of care quality, parental economic status, maternal marital status, and maternal education."

Once again it is possible to read the research in many different ways. And once again the question for parents is, "Do you want to take the risk?" On a logical basis it would seem that the more time the infant spends with its caring mother, the stronger the attachment will be. Given the problems with daycare discussed in the sections above it does not seem likely that an infant could obtain the same quality of care in a childcare center as it could at home with its mother. While the negative effects of daycare on secure attachment might be relatively minor at first, they might make a major difference to adolescents or adults in terms of how they relate to others or how fully they use their potential.

Consider the shy child. Jerome Kagan showed that shyness is an inherited trait and that these children tend to be subdued and restrained in new situations. Daycare is definitely a new and potentially frightening situation for these children and it would be much more difficult for them to adjust to it than it would for more outgoing kids. Daycare could easily exacerbate the difficulties that shyness would create for these children in social situations, making them even shyer. If parents choose to accept only the most optimistic of the research interpretations, and cheerfully place their infant in daycare, they may never know what their child could have achieved later in life had the original parent-child attachment been stronger. Why take the chance?

## Hitting the Bottle

We have already noted that because mothers are generally responsible for feeding their babies, they help to develop the attachment between them. This is especially true when the mother breastfeeds. The warmth and body contact that mothers have during this feeding process are far greater than when a baby is bottle-fed. If an infant is placed in daycare, the mother is not even doing all the bottle-feeding. Instead a daycare worker is responsible for at least two feedings a day, and it is unlikely to be the same worker each time. No bonding with the mother will be occurring during these sessions, which is very likely to result in a weaker maternal attachment overall.

The desire of mothers to distance themselves from breastfeeding is not new. The example was originally set as far back as 600 BCE by Egyptian, Roman, and Greek royalty, who employed nursing mothers as wet nurses to do their job for them. Apparently breastfeeding was not a "royal" activity. This example was passed down for generations and was widely employed by the nobility of Europe until the late 1800s.

In the late 1800s, a belief in scientific triumph led people to believe that scientists could do better than Mother Nature, so they developed formulas to replace breast milk. The public eagerly accepted this, because it meant that the wealthier could again avoid the mess and bother of breastfeeding, and do it even more cheaply than by employing a wet nurse. And anyone could dry feed. No longer was it necessary to hire women who were already nursing babies. Within the medical profession the new specialty of pediatrics arose, simply to cope with the demand for infant formulas.

The trend to bottle-feeding was further encouraged by the need in both world wars for women to enter the workforce. This was particularly true during the Second World War, when there was a huge demand for "Rosie the Riveter" to take the place of "G.I. Joe." Not being able to breastfeed on the production line, women naturally turned to the bottle as a necessary substitute. Even after the war, when women returned to the home, the foundations of the women's movement had been set and the image of the breastfeeding mother, tied down to her home and baby, remained out of fashion. As a new generation of women entered the workplace in the 1960s and 1970s, there was little room for breastfeeding at work, so the babysitter's bottle replaced this practice.

A more sinister influence against breastfeeding has been the relatively effective lobby and campaigning of the formula manufacturers themselves. Until 1981, their products were advertised as being just as effective as breast milk itself for the health of babies. Those mothers who did not really want the hassles of breastfeeding, and many who were just unsure, were delighted to think that these claims were true. Fortunately, the breastfeeding advocates have fought back. One of their most important gains was the Code for the Marketing of Breast Milk Substitutes, sponsored by the World Health Organisation (WHO) and the United Nations Children's Fund (UNICEF) and implemented in 1981. With this code, infant formula companies were instructed not to promote their products as substitutes for breast milk. It eventually led to infant formula labels advising that "breast milk is best for babies up to two years."

The facts are very clear. Breastfeeding is not only important for the development of the mother-child bond but is vital to the good health of the child. According to the American Academy of Pediatrics the following benefits are obtained by the baby from breastfeeding:

- decreased incidence and severity of diarrhea, lower respiratory infection, otitis media (ear infections), bacteremia, bacterial meningitis, botulism, urinary tract infection, and necrotizing enterocolitis

- possible protection against sudden infant death syndrome, insulin-dependent diabetes mellitus, Crohn's disease, ulcerative colitis, lymphoma, allergic diseases, and other chronic digestive diseases

- possible enhancement of cognitive development, with some studies indicating a gain in IQ of up to 8 points

There are also beneficial effects to the mother, according to the same source. These include:

- increased levels of oxytocin, resulting in less postpartum bleeding and more rapid uterine involution; lactational amenorrhea causes less menstrual blood loss over the months after delivery

- earlier return to prepregnancy weight levels

- delayed resumption of ovulation with increased child spacing

- improved bone remineralization postpartum with reduction in hip fractures in the postmenopausal period

- reduced risk of ovarian cancer and premenopausal breast cancer

Despite all these proven advantages, the word does not seem to be going out to the medical doctors or, for some reason, they are not passing on the information they have to their patients. While there appears to have been an increase in the incidence of breast-feeding since the early 1990s, the figures are still discouraging. According to the Mothers Survey undertaken by the Ross Products Division of Abbot Laboratories, the prevalence of breastfeeding in American hospitals reached 67 percent in 1999. Thirty-one percent of mothers were still breastfeeding their infants at 6 months of age and 17 percent were still breastfeeding them at 1 year of age. This is compared to the U.S. Surgeon General's stated Goal for Healthy People 2010, which hopes to have 75 percent of women breastfeeding at hospital discharge and 50 percent breastfeeding at six months. In Canada the figures are similar. According to one study, 83 percent of babies were being breastfed at birth, but by 9 months only 19 percent of infants were still on the breast. Another study found that 86 percent of infants were initially breastfed, but this figure dropped to just over 40 percent after 6 months.

Since the great majority of pregnant mothers in Canada and the United States consult a physician during their gestation period, it is astounding that these figures are still this low. The damage being done to children's mental and physical health by mothers not breastfeeding is impossible to calculate. Take the prevalence of allergies for example. According to *allergies.about.com*, from 1990 to 1994, the number of people with self-reported asthma in the U.S. increased from 10.4 million to 14.6 million. Reports from Malaysia and the United Kingdom also show this alarming increase. While many factors are probably involved, the low incidence of breast-feeding is likely one of them.

Throughout the world experts are virtually unanimous in their agreement that breastfeeding is best for children, but disagree some-what on the recommended duration. According to the 1997 Breastfeeding Policy Statement of the American Academy of Pediatrics, it is recommended that breastfeeding continues for at least 12 months, and thereafter for as long as mutually desired. A more conservative approach is that of the World Health Organization,

.Possibly the most important aspect of nursing a toddler is not the nutritional or immunologic benefits, important as they are. I believe the most important aspect of nursing a toddler is the special relationship between child and mother. Breastfeeding is a life affirming act of love. This continues when the baby becomes a toddler. Anyone without prejudices, who has ever observed an older baby or toddler nursing can testify that there is something almost magical, something special, something far beyond food going on. A nursing toddler will sometimes spontaneously break into laughter for no obvious reason. His delight in the breast goes far beyond a source of food. And if the mother allows herself, breastfeeding becomes a source of delight for her as well, far beyond the pleasure of providing food. Of course, it's not *always* great, but what is? But when it is, it makes it all so worthwhile.

**Handout #21. *Toddler Nursing.* January 1998**
**Written by Jack Newman, MD, FRCPC**

which recommended in March 2000 that breastfeeding be continued for "about 6 months." Note that WHO looked only at the physiological benefits of mother's milk for children, and not at the psychological enrichment that the experience of breastfeeding provides. The words of Canada's leading authority on breastfeeding, Dr. Jack Newman, quoted in the above insert, sum it up best.

In short, the attachment between mother and child that is vital to the emotional health of children can be greatly aided by breastfeeding for at least the first year. Parents who choose to bottle-feed for this year, or who leave the feeding to daycare attendants, risk emotional damage to their children and at the same time miss out on a wonderful experience.

## What if Both Parents Have to Work?

After a recent television appearance, we received the following email:

### Subject: RE CKCO TV appearance

Dear Dr Wooding:
Further to your appearance on CKCO TV this evening, I
believe that although I agree with you on quite a number

of issues however I also believe that you are incorrect in a critical factor. Namely you infer that most, if not all, younger parents choose to work two jobs in order to live in large homes and purchase consumer goods.

Let me give you my experience and perhaps you can let me know how accurate your assessment is keeping in mind the constraints upon modern families. Both my wife and myself are university graduates raising three young children and this is our situation. As is the case of many university grads we have a mountain of student debts that we are trying to dig our way out of coupled with the cost of raising three young children. Are you aware that the cost of daycare alone for our three children is nearly $24,000 per year (after taxes)?

This fact, coupled with the inflationary pressures you alluded to (caused to a large degree by the feminist movement pushing large numbers of women into both higher education and the workforce) REQUIRES both parents of young families to work. Young Families are REQUIRED to work because, if they do not their families will be raised below the poverty line and the likelihood that they will own ANY house much less the large luxury ones that you talk of is virtually impossible.

If you doubt the accuracy of my statements look to studies by statistics Canada for young family incomes, and OSAP or other government student loan programs for the percentage of graduating students having difficulties with paying their debts (exceeding 25% if I am not mistaken).

We are doing our best to raise well disciplined children with manners, however the society in which we have chosen to do so has removed the support structures that were in place for the preceding generations.
Sincerely,
S_____

The writer makes several good points. There are many people who, because of economic circumstance, find that both parents must work. If these parents have tried everything in their power to try to keep one parent at home, then there is no choice. In the above case it must be assumed that the second parent is earning considerably more than $24,000 a year if the cost of placing their three children in childcare is to be covered with money left over to pay down their debts and to pay their monthly expenses.

Still, we can ask certain questions about their situation. Is there any chance that one parent could work from home? Could the main wage earner find a job in a city or town where the cost of a house is considerably lower? Could they get by with a less expensive vehicle? In other words, before deciding that both parents have to work, they need to exhaust every possible avenue for enabling one to stay home.

Dr. Laura Schlessinger took this position in an interview in 2004. She explained that when families believe that it is in the best interest of their children to be parented by a parent, they make it happen, no matter what the economy is doing at the time. They either scale down their standard of living or move to a place that's more economically friendly.

Dr. Laura's ideas are right on the money. Many people who think that both parents have to work have not explored all of their options—or more likely they are not prepared to make the lifestyle changes that these sacrifices might require. Driving a beater of a car instead of a new SUV is definitely a sacrifice. So is buying a fixer-upper in an older neighborhood rather than a brand new home in the suburbs. In many cases it is simply a matter of how important parents believe their children are, as opposed to the more material things of life. The email quoted below illustrates this point.

> I heard about you on the news. I just wanted to tell you my experience of raising kids. I stayed home with my kids.
> I loved raising kids; it was so much fun. My husband and myself spent a lot of time with our kids. I started a part time job and based it around when my kids were in school. I was at home when they came home from school.

Anyways, I want to let you know ... I spent a lot of time with my kids, maybe too much. But they turned out stable, very polite, motivated adults. They have never tried drugs and do not drink. They are in university and are doing very well. But, I also want to tell you that when I stayed home with them, I had a lot of pressure from people that I should be working. I hated that; I wanted to raise my kids and did not want someone else to.

It makes a difference ... They are happy and very out-going. It does make a difference. Everyone needs to know someone cares about them and that they are there for them throughout everything life brings upon them. I am very close with my kids and I think the world of them.

What I have noticed about people today is that they are so materialistic and forgot to care about people in general. They might have all the material goods but have other prob-lems that are far greater to deal with like emotional and behavioral problems. I have nothing in material, but I have a lot of love for people and my kids.

That is what the world is all about. I have the respect of my kids and their love and concern.

Parenting does make a difference.

Mary _____

At the very least, mothers should try to stay home for the first year of the child's life. Still, if all possible attempts to make it eco-nomically possible for one parent to stay at home with the kids have been tried, and the finances still do not work, then there is little choice but for both parents to work. This certainly happens. At this point, it does not help for self-righteous "experts" to add to the pressure these parents already feel by throwing statistics at them. If childcare is the only answer to make life work, then the best approach would be to try to avoid the major daycare centers and find a caring person who wants to look after some children to ease her own financial burdens. The combination of a low caregiver-child ratio and a caring personality will be far better for the kids than a large for-profit center and will help to minimize any negative effects of not having a real parent around.

More important, in these cases it is essential that parents spend as much time as possible with the children when they are at home. The kids must become a priority, ahead of hobbies, committees, and even housecleaning. Both parents must be heavily involved with their children as often as possible. Such active parenting is not a burden, but, as Mary says above, it is fun and rewarding.

In sum, we refer to the subtitle of one of Dr. Laura's books on parenting, *Don't Have Them If You Won't Raise Them*. If parents decide to have children, they should also decide to raise their children themselves. There are too many potential risks if they do not and almost none if they do.

## What Should Our Governments Be Doing?

It is this author's belief, then, that the majority of children today are placed into daycare situations because of the mistaken values of their parents. Either they are actively pursuing affluence and the acquisition of possessions or they believe that it is more important for a mother to fulfill her career potential, while still allowing dad to work, than it is to raise their own children. These are choices that parents make, often by just going with the flow of contemporary thought rather than by doing the research necessary to make the best decisions for their children. The past two chapters have clearly explained why these approaches can potentially harm their children, causing them greater stress throughout their lives. There is little reason, therefore, for governments to use tax dollars to support these faulty decisions. Unfortunately that is exactly what has been happening.

To date the pressure on governments, from parents, women's interest groups, and daycare owners has been for subsidies and tax breaks so that parents can put their children into daily childcare. This is obviously not the right approach. Instead, governments must play a role in helping one parent stay at home with the children.

There are 3 ways that governments can do this: through increased maternity leave, by removing taxation inequities, and by changing pension benefit calculations for stay-at-home parents. Let's explore these three policy issues.

## 1. Maternity Leave

If society wants to encourage mothers to stay at home with their children for at least the child's first year, governments must provide paid maternity leave. To date, Sweden appears to have the most generous policy in this area as it allows 16 months of paid maternity leave per child, with the cost shared equally between the employer and the state. In Canada, mothers are allowed 50 weeks of maternity leave, during which the Mom is paid Employment Insurance by the government. The United Kingdom offers only 13 weeks maternity leave per child, but is presently considering raising it to a full year.

And then there is the United States. Maternity leave in the U.S. varies from state to state. Paid maternity leave is rare in the U.S. There are some companies that provide new parents with limited paid leave, which can encompass up to six weeks. Such restrictions have forced some parents to use a combination of short-term disability, sick leave, vacation, personal days, and unpaid family leave to extend their leave from two to four months. This is an awkward system and is highly unfair to those who either do not have short-term disability policies or medical insurance of any kind. Actual state laws vary from no maternity leave, to six weeks, in the case of California. In 2004, California became the first state to offer paid family leave. Californians will be able to take an additional six weeks of family leave at partial pay after their six weeks of short-term disability runs out. Paid family leave bills have been introduced in other states as well.

> It's not just a matter of helping parents with the economic burdens of raising kids. We're talking about giving the important work a new measure of status and respect.
>
> **U.S. National Parenting Association**

If tax dollars are to be used in any way to support parents, the first step should be for everyone to have access to a full year's paid maternity leave so that mothers can breastfeed and care for their infants in this critical time period.

## 2. Changes to the Tax System

In Canada, the present system of taxation is based on individuals, rather than families. This encourages two people to work, because it gives working parents more disposable income than they would have if they were taxed as a family. For example, if both parents are making around $50,000 and taxed as if they were making $100,000, then they would pay over $25,000 in federal and provincial taxes. As it is, they pay only $20,228 by being taxed as if they were single. Parents are also allowed to deduct up to $7000 for each child for childcare expenses. On the other hand, there are no tax deductions (other than the spousal amount) for the mother that stays at home, looking after the children but earning no income.

In the U.S. the savings are similar as the above individuals would pay about $10,000 each, while if taxed on the combined total it would amount to about $24,600. These figures clearly show that there are considerable tax benefits involved when both parents work.

A more effective system might involve a family tax rate that does not just give a token spousal deduction for a dependant, but makes it clearly worthwhile for one parent to stay at home to raise the children. Once the children were in school, the tax rate could revert back to the individual system. For this to happen, however, governments would have to be convinced that having a parent stay home with the children is of benefit to the country. At present the opposite case has been presented. In Canada, parents are allowed to deduct a maximum of $14,000 for childcare. The combination of the individual tax rate with this generous deduction makes it highly attractive financially for both parents to work. In the U.S. tax law does not allow a standard amount that can be deducted for childcare expenses, but federal law does allow, as a credit against tax, a percentage of the child and dependant care expenses—if the parents can show that these expenses are necessary for them to be gainfully employed. The amount of qualifying expenses for the credit is limited to $2,400 for one dependant ($4,800 for two or more), and the amount ranges from 20 percent to 30 percent. This is not nearly as generous as Canada's deduction, but bills are pending to create a deduction similar to it.

What this means is that the daycare lobby has been far more effective than parent-friendly organizations in reaching the ears of Canadian and American legislators. In light of present research, the entire tax structure should be reviewed to better support parents who want to raise their children themselves.

## 3. Pension Review

The third policy shift necessary for more parents to stay at home with their children is a review of pension benefit credits. Currently, stay-at-home parents do not contribute to their pension plans during these years and therefore get no credit for this time when retirement arrives. This reduces their pension. Governments must introduce legislation to remedy this situation, perhaps by allowing five years of pension credit per child, with a formula for overlapping children. In other words, in a family where the two children are two years apart in age, the parents would receive a total of seven years pension credit for whichever parent stayed at home, thus redressing the present pension deficit.

For too long now daycare has not been subject to critical debate, either within families or among society as a whole. In the light of the research now available it is clear that daycare is harming children and creating more stress in their lives. This is not necessary, except among those who truly cannot afford to do otherwise. For the majority of the population, however, it is time to begin to question this "sacred cow" and to pay attention to the short-term and long-term impacts on children, their families, and our society.

# CHAPTER IV

# Divorce

Until recently divorce was another subject that, like daycare, brooked no dissent. If people were unhappy in their marriages, it was assumed that they should divorce. Life was short, and happiness was paramount. Unfortunately, this attitude, which evolved over many years, had an unforeseen downside: it hurt any children involved. Those who worked closest with children, such as teachers, social workers, and counselors, watched the negative effects divorce had on children, but those wishing to divorce did not want to hear that their actions would have negative consequences. They wanted to believe that their personal happiness was too important to submerge for the years that their children were growing up, and they not only ignored any naysayers who said otherwise, they actively sought reassurance that their course of action was the right one. Generally, however, it was not. Divorce has become a key contributor to the high stress levels of today's children, and a major cause of the high levels of youth violence, emotional disturbances, and drug use.

> "The worst reconciliation is better than the best divorce."
>
> **Miguel de Cervantes Saavedra,** author of *Don Quixote*

## The History of Divorce

The trend towards divorce on demand has been slow but steady in North America ever since the United States and Canada were first colonized. The U.S. has consistently led in the liberalization of divorce laws as a result of the principles on which the country was originally founded, the rights of the individual. Divorce legislation in that country was enacted by many states soon after independence was obtained from Great Britain. As early as the 1780s, Connecticut and Massachusetts permitted divorce on such grounds as adultery, fraudulent contract (such as representing yourself as having more assets than actually existed), and desertion for three years or prolonged absence with the presumption of death. Connecticut added two more grounds in 1843, habitual drunkenness and intolerable cruelty. These laws were expanded even further in 1849 to include life imprisonment, any infamous crime involving a violation of conjugal duty, and "any such misconduct as permanently destroys the happiness of the petitioner and defeats the purpose of the marriage relation."

While for many years Connecticut had the most liberal divorce laws, California and the western states eventually caught up. The Gold Rush of 1848 contributed to liberalization of California divorce law as there was a scarcity of women and they apparently wanted the option of selecting the best (or richest) man and, for some reason the legislators went along with this. In 1851 the state enacted its first divorce law, which included such grounds as impotence, adultery, extreme cruelty, desertion or neglect, habitual intemperance, fraud, and conviction for a felony.

Throughout the nineteenth century, grounds for divorce continued to be expanded throughout the states. By 1900 most states had adopted four major elements of divorce law: fault based grounds, one party's guilt, the continuation of gender-based marital responsibilities after divorce, and the linkage of financial awards to findings of fault. These elements show that the process of divorce had become a sophisticated and complex process that took into account whose fault the divorce was and levied compensation for the person left responsible for the children—usually the mother.

Despite the gradual liberalization of the divorce laws, the incidence of divorce remained low throughout the United States; those who did divorce, especially women, were usually stigmatized. Much of this could be credited to the powerful influence of religion. Neither the Protestant nor the Catholic churches accepted the concept of divorce, and both actively preached against it, most likely because of its negative effects on children and its impoverishing effects on females.

In Canada, the only grounds for divorce was adultery, except in Nova Scotia where cruelty was also accepted as grounds for the dissolution of a marriage. In 1925, the federal government took over from the provinces the responsibility for administering the divorce laws, but retained infidelity as the main grounds for divorce. While the federalizing of divorce proceedings might have reduced the costs of divorce, it was still a rare phenomenon. To go to court and publicly admit to being unfaithful was an anathema to most adulterers and humiliating for the cuckolded spouse. Most couples found that there was little choice but to stay together, so they did.

In 1968 Canada liberalized the divorce laws to include the new grounds of marital breakdown (separation for three years) as well as infidelity and cruelty. This was basically a no-fault divorce option that was eagerly accepted by a generation that was coming to value individual freedoms. Similar changes were enacted by the Reagan government in California one year later and the no-fault era was underway.

## The Incidence of Divorce

The following two graphs show the historical trends in divorce. The impact of the no-fault legislation is apparent in both graphs. Note the huge rise in divorce incidence in Canada in 1970 and thereafter, once the "marital separation" clause had been added to the Divorce Act, and a similar sharp rise in the U.S. rate between 1970 and 1975.

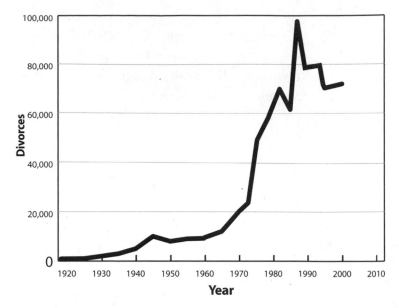

Fig. 1: Divorces in Canada 1921–2001 – **Historical Statistics of Canada: Section B. Vital Statistics and Health 11-516-XIE, Health Statistics Division.**

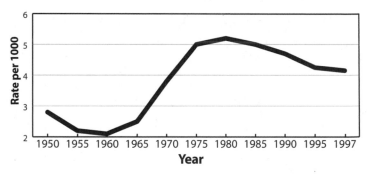

Fig. 2: US Marriage and Divorce Rates (per 1000 population) from 1950–1997

Both graphs show a significant spike following World War II after couples had been separated for long periods of time, allowing affection to wither and new relationships to form. This quickly dropped off again following a short period of stability, although never back to the prewar rates. Then, slowly at first then in a flood, the divorce rates resumed their rise. As the graphs show, in a space of just over 50 years, the divorce rate rose dramatically. Divorces became so frequent and have become so common that it is now readily accepted as a normal aspect of modern society.

Statistics bear witness to the impact of the no-fault divorce legislation. Of the Canadian couples who married in 1968-69, 11 percent were divorced before their tenth wedding anniversary. Of those who married in 1973-74, 14 percent did not make it to their tenth anniversary. The 10-year divorce rate rose to 18 percent for those married in 1983-84. By 1996, 37 percent of Canadian marriages were expected to end in divorce. The situation has been even worse in the United States where, the divorce rate rose from 27 couples out of every 100 who married in 1969 to the present rate of 51 out of 100. In gambler's terms, the chances are that 45 percent of first marriages will break up and a whopping 60 percent of second marriages will fail.

These figures raise the question as to why public pressure on politicians became so great that the divorce laws were liberalized in both countries at the same time, causing the skyrocketing of the divorce rates and acceptance of divorce as a fact of modern life?

## The Origins of the Divorce Culture

Most authorities trace the roots of the divorce culture to the Second World War. The heavy drain on industrial manpower caused by the armed forces resulted in women, as personified by "Rosie the Riveter," being called on to fill traditionally male jobs. Suddenly women had independence, both financially and emotionally, that they had never had before. Even though most settled back into the more traditional roles of wife and mother after the war, the mold had been broken and the taste of freedom and independence that working gave women lingered into the 1960s. At this point several other forces developed that changed modern society radically.

## The Forces of the 1960s

In her 1996 book, *The Divorce Culture*, Barbara Dafoe Whitehead describes two types of divorce: instrumental divorce and expressive divorce. Prior to the 1960s, "instrumental divorce" was practiced by wealthy socialites, business tycoons, and movie stars. Such people tended to view marriage as a means of upward mobility, to gain publicity, or to improve their financial or social standing. Love and affection may not have been involved, and if a better "opportunity" came along, then divorce from the present spouse was the answer. Despite the prominence of these divorces and the publicity attached to them, instrumental divorce did not catch on with the wider public, who saw it as a circumstance related to wealth and fame.

In the 1960s, Whitehead argues, "expressive divorce" came into vogue. Whitehead uses this term to describe the trend whereby people used "the language of expressive individualism to describe their divorces." Many divorced people reported that divorce gave them a new-found sense of freedom and control over their personal lives. Several factors contributed to this trend. Post-war affluence raised people's expectations as to what they should have in life. As people worried less about their financial status, they had time to review their personal happiness. Many looked at their marriages and found, that despite the material accumulations, they remained personally unhappy. Meanwhile, social movements such as the Civil Rights Movement, the anti-Vietnam war protests, and the women's movement all sought to challenge traditional establishment institutions. For many, marriage was the embodiment of such an establishment institution, and became a target for ridicule and rejection. Finally, the emergence of the "me" generation, with a culture that emphasized personal happiness above all else, argued against the need to be "stuck" in an unhappy marriage. If a person was not happy, then they should look for ways to reacquire a happier state, and if their marriage was the problem, then it should be ended, despite the possible negative effects on any children.

According to Judith Wallerstein, writing in *The Unexpected Legacy of Divorce*, two key myths arose from this "me" type of thinking that further helped to legitimize divorce. The first was that if parents are happier, their children will be happier too. Under this myth, children may be initially distressed by the divorce, but because they are *resilient*, they will soon recover. The second myth identified by Wallerstein is that divorce is a temporary crisis that only has major effects on parents and children around the time of the breakup. While there may be temporary adjustment problems, under this myth there are no long-term effects.

This logic might have some credibility if the breakup was very amicable and there was never any rancor or ill-will between the parents, if there was no change in financial status, if the parents were able to convince the children that they were no way at fault, if the parents lived very close to each other, and if they never had another relationship of any kind. There are so many "ifs" in this last sentence that it leaves one breathless. Basically, this never actually happens, and frankly, if the parents could work all these details out, they would probably have the skills to stay together in the first place.

Both of these myths developed because parents really wanted to believe that their happiness was paramount and there were no real reasons for not pursuing this happiness. Given that there was no research available on the long-term effects of divorce on children, these myths not only gained credibility, they became very hard to break when the research finally became available many years later.

## The Women's Movement and Divorce

In a 1974 speech, Betty Friedan said, "If divorce has increased by one thousand percent, don't blame the women's movement. Blame the obsolete sex roles on which our marriages were based." Friedan appears to argue that the women's movement should not be blamed

## The Delayed Effects of Divorce

Bill and Shelley were both professionals who divorced when their children were very young. They seemed to have handled the divorce perfectly. They communicated well, they lived close together, there were no custody hassles and he provided adequate child support. The children seemed perfectly happy to go back and forth between both homes and there were no outward signs of any distress on their part for several years. Then their children became teenagers.

Suddenly the 14-year-old son was getting angry with both parents over very minor issues, far out of proportion to the seriousness of the original problem. He also began suffering bouts of depression that caused him to periodically refuse to go to school.

After several sessions with a psychologist it transpired that he was very angry with his dad for (as he saw it) leaving the family. It was virtually a delayed reaction to a divorce that had happened several years earlier.

No sooner were his problems under control than the daughter also began refusing to go to school. This also required therapy and again the underlying cause was anger at the father.

These delayed reactions were not foreseen by the originators of the divorce myths detailed by Judith Wallerstein.

for the rapidly rising divorce rate, but in fact shows that it certainly played a role in encouraging women to be dissatisfied with their lot in life. The second wave of feminism, of which Friedan was one of the leaders, promoted self-fulfillment for women as much as it attempted to redress the many inequities that existed between men and women in our society. The movement suggested that men had deliberately created most of these inequities and that there was a virtual male conspiracy to keep women in their place—the home. Consider the following quotations:

> The institution of marriage is the chief vehicle for the perpetuation of the oppression of women; it is through the role of wife that the subjugation of women is maintained. In a very real way, the role of wife has been the genesis of women's rebellion throughout history.
> Marlene Dixon (1969)

[Wives'] chattel status continues in their loss of name, their obligation to adopt the husband's domicile and the general legal assumption that marriage involves an exchange of the female's domestic service and [sexual] consortium in return for financial support.

Kate Millett (1969)

*The nuclear family must be destroyed,* and people must find better ways of living together ... Whatever its ultimate meaning, the break-up of families now is an objectively revolutionary process ... Families have supported oppression by separating people into small, isolated units, unable to join together to fight for common interests.

Linda Gordon (1969)

The effect of views such as those of Friedan, Dixon, and Millett, even if they were not accepted completely, was to give another reason for people dissatisfied with their marriages to bail out of them. The second wave of the women's movement had its major influence in the 1970s and, together with the influences of the social movements of the 1960s, helped to make divorce acceptable for those in unhappy marriages. Most feminists did not consider any effects that divorce might have on children; they were only concerned about the "subjugation" of women, what they felt was a major cause of their lowly status in life.

As discussed in Chapter II, many of the concerns of the women's movement had considerable validity and needed to be addressed. But by devaluing marriage as a whole, rather than just seeking to redress the inequities, the feminist writers tended to encourage women to throw off the shackles of their unhappy marriage to seek happiness and fulfillment, no matter what the consequences might be to their children.

## The Failure of Organized Religion

Until the socially active 1960s religion played an important role in most North American families. The active opposition of Protestant and Roman Catholic churches acted as a deterrent to family breakups. One of the consequences of the social upheaval of the 1960s, however, was the decline in the authority of the church. As well, many Protestant churches also fell prey to the social liberalization of the period. Both trends affected the growth of divorce. As noted by David Blankenhorn, since that time "many religious leaders—especially in the mainline Protestant denominations—have largely abandoned marriage as a vital area of religious attention, essentially handing the entire matter over to opinion leaders and divorce lawyers in secular society." Similarly with the Catholic Church, which although did not soften its stand on divorce, had seen its sense of authority erode with the social liberalization of the 1960s. The result was that churches could not help but stem the tide of divorce, and the breakup of families continued its acceleration.

For many years, the longitudinal research to counter modern thinking about divorce was simply unavailable. Such research is now emerging, but because the ideas and myths of this divorce culture are now so firmly entrenched, it is extremely difficult to correct the erroneous thinking.

## The Effects of Divorce on Children

As mentioned above, the growing acceptance of divorce as an integral part of our society has led to the development of a major myth about its effects on children outlined by Judith Wallerstein. Divorcing parents want to believe that their children will suffer no ill effects from the breakup of the family or, if there are any effects, they will be temporary in nature.

For many years unhappily married parents have believed that because their children are young, they can "bounce back" from the disappointments of their parents divorcing. A word for this has even been coined—"resilience." Parents want to believe that their kids are resilient and will quickly recover from any emotional trauma.

This is simply not the case. A recent monumental study by Patrick F. Fagan and Robert Rector, called "The Effects of Divorce on America" clearly shows the negative effects that divorce has on children. By surveying over two hundred research studies on this topic, they concluded that these effects are far more serious than even the most pessimistic researchers might have believed just a few years ago. Divorce, they show, impacts all areas of a child's life:

- **Physical:** Children whose parents have divorced are increasingly the victims of abuse and neglect. They exhibit more health problems, as well as behavioral and emotional problems. They are more frequently involved in crime and drug abuse, and have higher rates of suicide. They even have shorter life spans.

- **Educational:** Children of divorced parents frequently do poorly in school. They perform more poorly than their peers from intact two-parent families in reading, spelling and mathematics. They are also more likely to repeat a grade and to have higher dropout rates and lower rates of graduation.

- **Financial:** Divorce generally reduces the income of the child's primary household and seriously diminishes the potential of every member of the household to accumulate wealth. For families that were not poor before the divorce, the drop in income can be as much as 50 percent. This decline in income is also intergenerational, since children whose parents divorce are likely to earn less as adults than children raised in intact families.

- **Spiritual:** Religious worship, which has been linked in many studies to health and happiness, longer lives, longer marriages and a better family life, is less prevalent in divorced families.

- **Familial:** Divorce permanently weakens the relationship between a child and his or her parents.

- **Sexual:** Children of divorce tend to lose their virginity earlier, cohabit more frequently, have higher divorce rates later in life, and have less desire to have children.

- **Social:** Divorce diminishes the capacity of children to handle conflict. For example, compared with students from intact families, college students from divorced families use violence more frequently to resolve conflict. Children from divorced families, both male and female, are more likely to be aggressive and physically violent with their friends.

- **Emotional:** Divorce leaves most children feeling emotionally insecure, with a poorer self-image. Children in a divorced family are also more likely to believe that the social environment is unpredictable and uncontrollable. This results in poor social skills and often rejection by the peer group. Children of divorce tend to have fewer friends and to complain more about the lack of support they receive from the friends they have.

> "There are psychological, emotional, economical and physical costs related to these separations. Children living in these environments really don't learn much about harmony and what it takes to make a happy, successful relationship."
>
> **Dr. Harold Minden, Professor Emeritus, York University (2000)**

- **Romantic:** The divorce of parents makes romance and courtship more difficult for children as they reach adulthood. The older teenagers and young adults date more often, have more failed romantic relationships, and tend to have shorter relationships with their dating partners. *These effects on relationships seem to be the strongest when the divorce takes place during the teenage years.*

Note that the frightening results were not obtained from a single research study, but from an analysis of the results of over 200 studies by many of the most respected researchers in the world in the area of divorce and its effects on children. Since this paper was released in 2000, several other major works have been published that confirm these findings. The titles of such works make clear the message: *A Generation at Risk: Growing Up in an Era of Family Upheaval*; *The Case for Marriage: Why Married People Are Happier, Healthier, and Better Off Financially*; *For Better or Worse: Divorce Reconsidered*; *Life Without Father: Compelling New Evidence That Fatherhood and Marriage Are Indispensable for the Good of Children and Society*; *The Love They Lost: Living With the Legacy of Our Parents' Divorce*; and *The Unexpected Legacy of Divorce: A 25 Year Landmark Study.*

There can be little doubt that divorce is the major contributor to the increase in stress of today's youth. An interesting trend can be seen by comparing the graph of the divorce rate in the U.S. to a graph of the youth violence in that country. This comparison clearly shows that just a few years after the peak in the U.S. divorce rate (around 1980), the arrest rates for violent crimes started to rise. In other words, the higher rate of divorce correlates to the higher levels of teenage violence. Given what we now know about the effects of divorce on children, it seems obvious that, while there are certainly other factors that could be contributing to this phenomenon, there is a relationship between the two variables of divorce and youth violence.

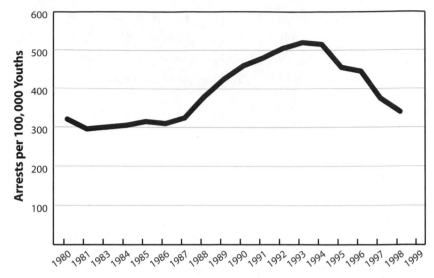

Fig. 3: Arrest rates of youth age 10-17 for serious violent crime, 1980-1999

## The Causes of Divorce Effects on Children

What is it about a divorce that causes such tremendous stress, in both the short and long terms, in children? As it turns out, there are a huge number of factors that produce this stress. Here are six main areas, as established by Paul Amato, co-author of *A Generation at Risk: Growing Up in an Era of Family Upheaval*, and others.

### 1. Parental Loss

Despite parental attempts to keep both of them in their children's lives, divorce often causes one of the parents, usually the father, to have a much diminished role in the day-to-day activities of the children. Equal joint custody rarely works for long, if attempted at all, and the children eventually lose the knowledge, skills, and emotional support of one of their parents. No matter how rancorous the breakup, the children generally love both parents and miss the one who departs. This could be particularly hard on boys, for example, who have more in common with their fathers—like sports and handyman activities—than their mothers. Similarly girls could miss their mothers for the same loss of common interests. There is an emotional letdown to a loved parent leaving the household that cannot be made up by one parent alone. While this loss might not be devastating to all children, it can certainly affect the more sensitive ones, and can be a major cause of insecurity and the inability to trust future relationships that has been seen to occur in many children of divorce.

If both parents could find some way to stay equally as involved with their children after the divorce, then perhaps no sense of loss need be felt. Unfortunately this is rarely the case. In far too many instances, divorced fathers (and occasionally mothers) fade completely from their children's lives within a very few years. One parent might remarry and become involved in a new family. The bitterness of the breakup and subsequent interparental conflict might lead one parent to stay away. Children themselves might feel anger toward one parent if they blame that parent for the divorce. Whatever the cause of this fade-out, children rarely rebound completely from the sense of abandonment it brings.

## 2. Economic Loss

Rarely can a single parent live as affluently as two parents can. The resulting drop in économic status, usually experienced by the custodial parent (most commonly the mother) brings with it many stresses in terms of constrained living quarters and a lack of money for clothing and extracurricular activities. Usually this requires the custodial parent to work all day, then be the sole parent at night. This extra strain often causes more stress on this parent, who passes it on to the children through a reduced store of patience and lowered frustration threshold. When the children become teenagers, their own moodiness can easily result in major battles with their frazzled parent.

In many divorced families, the custodial parent is often heard by the children lamenting the unwillingness (rarely the inability) of the estranged parent to contribute enough money to their support.

This can have two effects. Either it succeeds in convincing the children that their non-custodial parent is a cheapskate and makes them angry with that person, or it boomerangs and makes them upset with the custodial parent for disparaging the absent one. Rarely are the children able to stay neutral, so they end up angry with one loved one or the other. This situation puts children in a very unfair position, and adds greatly to the stresses of the divorce situation.

## 3. Increased Life Stress

Divorce disrupts all aspects of the lives of children. Often the family must change residences, meaning new schools and new friends. While younger children may adapt relatively easily to these location changes, teenagers have a far more difficult time. These older children rely on their friends for support in times of crisis. Removing them from this source of comfort just adds to the misery the breakup causes.

Divorce also changes previously stable relationships. In cases of angry breakups, it may make one set of grandparents unavailable, as the alienated spouse may enlist them to his or her side. The same applies to aunts, uncles, and cousins. At best the relationship is strained as the children and relatives must carefully avoid taking sides. Along with these strained relationships, holidays such as Christmas, Easter, and summer vacations become nightmarish as family traditions are shattered and careful planning must now be done to ensure the kids spend time with both parents. Instead of the whole family going out to select a Christmas tree, kids erect a Wal-Mart special in their mother's apartment, while dad might not even have a tree. Christmas day is fragmented, with the children leaving one residence to go to the other parent's domicile. Instead of enjoyable family occasions, holidays become hectic and stressful, and often dreaded by the children.

The visitation shuffle also adds stress to kids' lives. The constant moving back and forth from mom's to dad's usually works while the kids are young—it actually can be enjoyable having two bedrooms and two sets of toys—but becomes frustrating and disruptive as the children get older. Unless both residences are very close together, visitation means that kids are away from their friends for the period of the visit, and must leave the majority of their belongings in their primary residence. As teenagers get jobs, boy/girlfriends, and increased homework levels, the whole process becomes frustrating for them, and they begin to resist the visitation entirely. This in turn strains their relationship with the non-custodial parent.

Life for the children of divorce usually becomes even more stressful when one or both parents begin a new relationship. Rarely does mom's or dad's new friend understand the resentment that the children have for them. This resentment comes from the fact that the kids always want their parents to get back together again and a new relationship means that the likelihood of this happening is seriously diminished. This often results in the children being at best surly towards the new person and at worst openly hostile. Few adults understand this resentment and are either hurt by it or, more commonly, overreact to it with frustration, causing them to withdraw from trying to have a relationship with the kids. This puzzles the parent who may also overreact to the situation, trying to make the children behave in a more friendly fashion to the new person, when their instincts are telling them to do the opposite. The result is stress and strain for everyone.

This situation can worsen when the parent marries a new friend. Stepparents rarely understand how to deal with the natural resentment of the stepchildren. They often tend to be heavy on the discipline to try to get the children to shape up. This inevitably produces the opposite reaction and the classic "evil stepmother (or father)" effect results. To avoid the stress that stepparenting can produce, both parents and their new friends must exercise extreme caution in entering the relationship. They must understand that hostility from the children is normal and they must work hard to overcome it in as calm a manner as possible. Unfortunately, this rarely happens.

## 4. Poor Parental Adjustment

Divorce is often a nerve shattering experience for many adults. In cases where they did not see it coming (as in the case of adultery) or where one spouse is not psychologically capable of parenting on his or her own, the divorce can permanently disrupt family life. Single parenting takes its toll on even the strongest adults. More physical and psychological stamina is required because there is no one else available to help. It requires more organization, patience, and household structure. Unfortunately some people are not naturally able to cope with buying the food and clothing, repairing the household damage, making the lunches, disciplining the children, supervising their education, and coordinating the extracurricular activities. This results in household chaos and occasionally anarchy. A parent whose psychological health is damaged by the divorce process and cannot effectively manage a household creates tremendous stress within the family, especially as the children get older. Teenagers in all households try to discover their own identities by pushing limits. Those from divorced families have the added burdens of feeling rejected by or angry at the parent who left, of coping with related mood swings of other family members, or of dealing with a defensive stepparent. These teenagers become impossible to handle for a parent who is suffering from the psychological scars of the divorce, adding to everyone's already massive stress load.

It takes psychologically strong and well-organized people to single parent, or even to shared parent. If the divorce has left one parent traumatized, the parent should seek psychological help immediately or the children will suffer more from the results of the divorce than they already are.

## 5. Lack of Parental Competence

Some adults, divorced or single, just do not make effective parents. This may be the result of their own family history, of ineffective concepts of discipline, of mental health problems, or of gross disorganization. Whatever the cause, these parenting defects are often compensated for by their spouse, who tends to shoulder the majority of the parenting burden. When the marriage dissolves, whether the ineffective parent has custody or not, these defects become glaringly obvious and can set up some very stressful situations.

A classic example of this parental incompetence is the parent who does not understand the necessity for a sound discipline structure. When the children have no rules in one house (whether because the parent does not believe in it or because the parent is trying to soften the blow of the divorce for the kids), and the other parent is trying to maintain some discipline, the difference becomes too much for the kids. They cannot understand why the two households are so different and tend to blame the stricter parent for the problems. They have difficulty adjusting to the wide variation, and put pressure on the more discipline-oriented parent to loosen up. More often than not, the strict parent does loosen up, to the detriment of the children.

As will be discussed in the next chapter, children need discipline. They need to know where the boundaries are to feel secure and to feel that their parents do love them. While they initially enjoy their new-found freedom, this enjoyment eventually turns to frustration and anger, and they will push and push until they find the limits. If none are available, they can quickly become out of control.

Similarly, when one parent is constantly angry or depressed, the children add the parent's burden to their own. Eventually they will prefer to stay at the more competent parent's place full-time, yet feel guilty about wanting to do this. It places tremendous stress on young people who often do not realize why they feel as they do, only that they are unhappy.

It is difficult to do anything to remedy the situation of an incompetent parent, unless that parent realizes there is a problem and seeks help. Unfortunately this rarely happens until the situation is out of control and almost impossible to salvage.

## 6. Interparental Conflict

Divorce usually leaves one or both parents feeling bitter and angry. Even after the divorce, many try to get back at their former spouse through such tactics as withholding visitation rights, withholding support payments, bribing the children by buying them expensive gifts that they know their spouse can't match, or by criticizing their ex's in front of the children. What these parents are actually doing is using the children as weapons against their former spouse.

The exposure to this constant conflict is incredibly wearing on children who love both parents and do not understand what the fighting is all about. It puts them in the intolerable position of being forced to choose between parents whom they love equally, again adding to the stress that the divorce has already created.

### Parental Adjustment or Parental Incompetence?

When Aaron left Jennifer for another woman she was devastated. While the marriage had not been "made in heaven," it had seemed reasonably happy and their two children were doing well, both sociably and academically. This all changed when Aaron walked out. While their son had already left home, their daughter, Lisa, immediately began reacting to the separation. She became very belligerent to her father, who she blamed for the separation, but what was even more puzzling was her acting out at home. She began to come and go as she pleased, drink and use drugs and to get into trouble at school. This despite the fact that it was her father with whom she was angry.

Upon consulting a psychologist, it quickly became clear that Jennifer had taken the divorce very badly. She was highly emotional and, when confronted by her daughter's acting out, lectured her at length. She was completely unable to communicate with Lisa at all and failed to notice her needs for attention and affection, being so caught up in her own. Despite several sessions with the psychologist, the situation continued to deteriorate, as Jennifer was unwilling or unable to follow the therapist's suggestions. Eventually they terminated the therapy. Jennifer's inability to communicate with Lisa was either the result of the effects of the separation on her or, more likely, Aaron had been doing the bulk of the parenting until he left, exposing Lisa to her mother's inability to deal with her. Adding to Lisa's frustration was that her anger with her father prevented her from going to live with him. Unfortunately, a typical divorce situation!

It is amazing that adults cannot try to put their differences aside for the sake of the children but then, if they had been able to do that, maybe they would not have needed to divorce in the first place. Of all the listed causes of the effects of divorce on children, interparental conflict is the most devastating.

## Fathers and Divorce

Although divorce necessarily involves two parents, fathers typically have a far more difficult time than mothers, particularly when they do not gain custody of the children. In acrimonious divorces, custody battles can turn into bitter battles between mother and father. The custodial parent might withhold the children from seeing the other parent whenever possible. Such a battle can become so tiring that the non-custodial dads will give up and gradually fade from the picture.

Even in amicable divorce situations, where the parents are actually trying to do the best for the children, non-custodial fathers seem to be confused about how to fulfill their roles outside of a marriage situation. This confusion often translates into their becoming less involved in their children's lives. Dr. Kerry Daly of the University of Guelph is one of Canada's foremost researchers on fatherhood. He explains that "being in a marriage and parenting is sort of a packaged deal and so much of what fathers do with their children is mediated by the moms, so that when the relationship goes sour it's hard for men to reestablish a relationship with their kids separate from that dynamic." In other words, without the moms, fathers often do not know how to form and maintain a relationship with their children. There is also no history among men of asking for help to maintain these relationships without the mediation of the mother, and there are very few support organizations available even if they did.

Non-custodial fathers also fade out of the picture when they fail to keep involved with their children's daily activities. They need to attend games, recitals, and concerts, and be knowledgeable about their hobbies and friends. This requires considerable time and effort, a commodity that is scarce for many dads. This becomes even harder if mom is not cooperating in keeping dad informed about upcoming events. For some reason most single fathers seem to be weak at keeping track of this type of information, with the result that they are unaware of what is happening in their children's lives and have little to talk about when they do see them.

The problems that fathers face seem to increase when their children become teenagers. Teens require far more activity and stimulation than do younger children, and non-custodial fathers need to become extremely creative to keep them entertained. This involves considerable planning for outings and activities, and fathers do not seem to be very good at this. Teenagers also need more emotional support than most parents realize during this stage of their lives, and fathers definitely struggle with this role when they don't have the direct intervention of the mother.

Whether in divorce or in marriage, fathers play a vital role in the lives of their children, a role that they must take seriously. This means spending as much time as possible with the kids, taking an active role in disciplining them, helping mom with the planning of family activities, and sharing the household workload. No matter how efficient the mothers are or how tired and stressed the dads are, fathers have to assume an equal share in all aspects of the family. Fatherhood needs to become the important value it was a generation ago to reduce the stress on children and mothers alike, and to promote the emotional health of the children.

## Can Children Survive their Parent's Divorce?

While the research shows that most children will suffer in some way as a result of their parents' divorce, there are certainly those who will not. These are the so-called "resilient" ones who are like

Timex watches—they "take a licking and keep on ticking." Resilience is defined as a "set of qualities that foster a process of successful adaptation and transformation despite risk and adversity." Resilient children might be from families with mentally ill, alcoholic, abusive, or criminally involved parents, from war-torn communities, or even from divorced families, yet they turn their lives around and live successfully. Researchers, such as those in the Kauai Longitudinal Study, have found that resilient children share certain personal characteristics right from the beginning of their lives. According to this study, those in the Kauai research who turned out to be resilient possessed temperaments that worked in their favor and personalities that attracted favorable attention from at least one adult—a mentor—who responded to them with affection and interest, especially during the first year of life. For some these mentors are grandparents who stand in for absent or incompetent parents. Later in their lives these mentors are often teachers, who not only show these children that they care about them, but at the same time set high standards and give the kids opportunities for meaningful involvement and responsibility within the school.

The temperaments of a resilient child include:

- social competence—the resilient child effectively communicates problems and feelings

- problem solving skills—resilient children use their intellectual abilities to find solutions to their problems rather than giving up or depending on others to find solutions for them

- autonomy—these children do not seem to consider themselves to be victims but assume responsibility for their own lives

- sense of purpose and future—resilient kids appear to have an optimistic view of life and feel that their lives will work out well, despite the odds against them

These personal attributes seem to attract mentors, so that the mix of their personalities with the guidance of one or more adults seems to be the right combination to ward off the effects of family stress and turmoil.

It would be highly optimistic of parents on the verge of divorce to assume that everything will be fine for their children because their kids are resilient. Unfortunately, research shows that, at best, only about 25 percent of children actually are. Parents cannot assume that their children will survive the breakup without any emotional scarring on the basis of resilience alone. Still, Stephanie Marston, writing in *The Divorced Parent*, notes that parents can nurture happy and well-adjusted children after divorce if only they meet five basic needs. These are:

1. Children must be protected from the parents' disputes

2. Children must be free to love both parents

3. Parents must shift their roles from intimate partners to parenting partners

4. Children must have access to both parents without being placed in loyalty conflicts

5. Parents must recover from the trauma of divorce and rebuild their lives

While it is hard to argue with this formula for post-divorce parenting success, there is a major flaw in the argument. It assumes that parents will put their differences behind them and put the children's welfare first. If they could agree to do this they could probably also save their marriage in the first place. By deciding to divorce, most parents have already put their own needs first, and will likely be unable to make the necessary compromises, Marston suggests. These five principles require a degree of maturity and emotional stability possessed by few couples on the verge of divorce. Most divorcing adults are overwhelmed by emotions, such as anger or depression, and do not think rationally about their children's emotional health. Why not use any rationality and concern for the children more productively and put the effort into marriage counseling? It would be far better for the kids to make the necessary compromises within the marriage rather than trying to follow Marston's prescription from two separate households.

Returning to the question posed at the beginning of this section, the answer is a qualified yes, children can survive divorce with little or no psychological scarring if they are the resilient type, or if their parents carefully follow Stephanie Marston's rather optimistic formula. Unfortunately the chances of being resilient are not high and the chances of being mature and rational enough to follow Marston's five steps are even worse.

## Does Divorce Result in Happiness?

The whole purpose of getting a divorce is to end the pain and turmoil of a miserable marriage and to find personal happiness. Until recently few adults challenged the concept that ending an unhappy marriage will bring this sought-after satisfaction. In 2002, however, this concept was tested in a formal research study. Using data collected in the late 1980s and early 1990s in the National Survey of Families and Households (a nationally representative survey) to look at all spouses (645 spouses out of 5,232 married adults), the study looked at those participants who had originally rated their marriages as unhappy. When these same unhappily married adults were re-interviewed a second time after a five-year interim, their lives had taken many different paths: some had divorced or separated and some stayed married. Because marital strife takes a toll on psychological well-being, most people would expect that unhappily married adults who divorced would be better off, happier, less depressed, have greater self-esteem, and a stronger sense of personal mastery, compared to those who stayed married. The evidence showed otherwise. Unhappily married adults who divorced were no more happier than unhappily married people who stayed together.

The study found the following results:

• **Unhappily married adults who divorced or separated were no happier, on average, than unhappily married adults who stayed married.** Even unhappy spouses who had divorced and remarried were no happier, on average, than unhappy spouses who stayed married. This was true even after controlling for race, age, gender, and income.

• **Divorce did not reduce symptoms of depression for unhappily married adults, or raise their self-esteem, or increase their sense of mastery, on average, compared to unhappy spouses who stayed married.** This was true even after controlling for race, age, gender, and income.

• **The vast majority of divorces (74 percent) happened to adults who had been happily married five years previously.** In this group, divorce was associated with dramatic declines in happiness and psychological well-being compared to those who stayed married.

• **Unhappy marriages were less common than unhappy spouses.** Three out of four unhappily married adults were married to someone who was happy with the marriage.

• **Staying married did not typically trap unhappy spouses in violent relationships.** Eighty-six percent of unhappily married adults reported no violence in their relationship (including 77 percent of unhappy spouses who later divorced or separated). Moreover, 93 percent of unhappy spouses who avoided divorce reported no violence in their marriage five years later.

• **Two out of 3 unhappily married adults who avoided divorce or separation ended up happily married five years later.** Just 1 out of 5 unhappy spouses who divorced or separated had happily remarried in the same time period.

Perhaps most surprising, the unhappiest marriages reported the most dramatic turnarounds. Among those who rated their marriages as "very unhappy," almost 8 out of 10 who avoided divorce were happily married five years later.

While more research is necessary, both to confirm these findings and to find out why unhappy marriages turn around, these results are fascinating. They cast serious doubt on one of the major myths of the divorce culture. Divorce does not automatically result in happiness; in fact, it rarely does so. Conversely, the study clearly shows that those who stick out the difficult times are rewarded with a happier marriage. This is a truth that many of those in previous generations, when divorce was much more difficult, already knew.

In light of these results, and the overwhelming evidence that divorce hurts children, there seems to be almost no case for divorce.

Does this mean that those in unhappy marriages should simply stoically endure their misery? Of course not. Instead they should find a good marriage counselor or, at the very least, get some of the excellent books that are available, such as Dr. Phil McGraw's *Relationship Rescue* or John M. Gottman's *The Seven Principles for Making Marriage Work: A Practical Guide from the Country's Foremost Relationship Expert*, and take steps to remedy the problems. And there will always be circumstances under which divorce will be necessary. Paul Amato and Alan Booth, writing in *A Generation at Risk*, found that about one-third of marriages, those in which violence and abuse were common, needed to be ended and the children of these divorces seemed to do better once released from the tense and dangerous family situations.

The majority of marriages, however, do not involve abuse or violence and most should not be ended. If parents strive to fix the problems rather than simply ending the marriage, both they and their children will be happier.

The advent of the divorce culture in Canada and the United States has resulted in severely increased stress levels in the children of these divorces and yet has not improved the happiness levels of the divorced parents. Given these facts, it is time for pressure to be put on governments to end no-fault divorce legislation. A message must be given to parents that they bear a huge responsibility to their children. If the faulty thinking of the 1960s can result in the easing of divorce laws, then the more rational approach of this new millennium should result in a return to more conservative legislation. It would be even better if a new fad—staying together for the children—was to develop at the grassroots level, without the need for government interference. This is unlikely to happen, however, unless people begin to learn about and understand the implications of the growing body of research on this subject. When this happens, the divorce myths will explode and with it will explode one of the main contributors to the parenting crisis.

# CHAPTER V

# Education

*We are born weak, we need strength; helpless, we need aid; foolish, we need reason. All that we lack at birth, all that we need when we come to man's estate, is the gift of education.*

**—Jean-Jacques Rousseau (1712-1778)**

E ducation may indeed be the gift that gives us strength, wisdom, and reason as Rousseau so clearly said, but today's parents fail to understand that education is also a major source of stress in children. There are many sources of this stress. Schools create stresses, through overcrowding, busing, and budget cutbacks. More relevant for our discussion, however, are the educational stresses that parents themselves place on their children. By seeing children as miniature extensions of themselves, and by funneling their children into the same kinds of work ethic patterns that they are in, parents have turned children into "products" to be developed rather than people to be nurtured. The result is that parents have failed to educate their children in basic values.

## "Parenting as Product Development"

This phrase, coined by sociologist Dr. William Doherty of the University of Minnesota, refers to the modern phenomenon of parents trying to get the best from their children by virtually treating them as a product to be developed and marketed. Under the guise of wanting the best for their children, many parents are attempting to program their children's lives for success virtually from the cradle. This programming starts with parents manipulating their children's education to get them into the best schools, then moves into developing their talents in sports and other extracurricular activities. The drive to make their kids into success stories, for various reasons, has turned these youngsters into "trophy kids" whose achievements are held up for the world to see like bowling trophies displayed on a shelf. More often than not the result is not success but a stress load that causes the trophies to burn out before they reach the pinnacle their parents imagined for them.

## From Pre-School to Prep School

There seems to be a widespread belief among parents, largely unsupported by research, that getting a head start on the educational process will create a better student in the higher grades. The only evidence that research has found for this to date is for children raised in abject poverty. Even the highly touted "Mozart Effect" (see below) has no research evidence to support it.

> "Well let's face it: we are trying our darndest to turn even our very youngest kids' lives into copies of our wired selves. Parents, particularly those of the college-educated upper middle class are obsessed with producing high-performance children. In the process they're driving our politicians to greater educational accountability through testing, tougher standards and the teaching or harder, more complex skills and concepts, in lower grades."
>
> **John Borst, former president, Hall-Dennis Institute for Learner-Centred Education (2002)**

### The Mozart Effect

According to supporters (**www.mozarteffect.com**), the Mozart Effect "is an inclusive term signifying the transformational powers of music in health, education, and well-being. It represents the general use of music to reduce stress, depression, or anxiety; induce relaxation or sleep; activate the body; and improve memory or awareness. Innovative and experimental uses of music and sound can improve listening disorders, dyslexia, attention deficit disorder, autism, and other mental and physical disorders and injuries." The concepts are based on the writings of Dr. Alfred Tomatis in France in the late 1950s. Despite the fact that the concepts have been around for almost 50 years, there has never been any solid evidence that any of this works, but it has added to the myths about the effectiveness of pre-school education.

To this end the parents begin to develop their "product" by buying educational toys. Stores are full of all sorts of resources designed to improve young minds, including toys, books, and videos. The next step for these parents is to make sure their children are enrolled in a pre-school program. They are convinced that the earlier the kids master reading and math the stronger the student they will make in high school and university. Furthermore, not just any pre-school will do. Many parents seek ones with a reputation for academic excellence, to the point that there are waiting lists to get into these stellar institutions. Some parents put their kids on these waiting lists as soon as they are born. While these may be the extremists, they are definitely the tip of a growing iceberg of parents who fear that failure to get a good educational start will doom their children to academic mediocrity.

Perhaps one of the major drawbacks to this drive for academic excellence at the pre-school level is that it takes away from children's playtime. Many parents have even devalued play as almost a complete waste of time. A study done in 2001 confirmed this tendency when it showed that since the 1970s children have lost 12 hours per week in free time, including a 25 percent drop in play and a 50 percent drop in unstructured outdoor activities. According to many experts, including Alan Simpson, spokesman for the National Association for the Education of Young Children, play is a crucial part of how young children learn. Unstructured play, where adults are not supervising the activities, provides a crucial foundation for children to develop creativity, intellect, and emotional and social skills. Despite this knowledge parents are choosing to send their children to academically oriented pre-schools when there is no research evidence that being taught to read or do mathematics at an early age will translate into greater academic success later in the children's school career. The result is often stress on 4-year-old children to read when they are not yet ready and to succeed academically when they should be playing happily.

After their children complete pre-school, parents continue the search for the best possible education for their products by seeking the best school for them. Several trends have emerged in this regard. First is the preference of many financially sound parents for private school education for their children. These schools are seen as more academically rigorous than their public counterparts, with smaller classes and a more focused educational program. Such schools might be appropriate for some students, but many of the more mediocre students find the constant emphasis on academic success stressful. Parents, however, will often overlook these stresses because of the prestige associated with having a child in a "name" academy.

A second, newer trend has been for parents to choose charter schools for their kids. Charter schools are those started by groups of parents, within the public education system, for a specific purpose. This movement started in Minnesota in 1992, and quickly spread to 42 states and the District of Columbia. In Canada, only Alberta has thus far adopted this alternative although other provinces are giving the idea strong consideration. Charter schools might emphasize religion, while others might be for gifted children, for science studies, for the arts, or for one gender or the other. These schools are funded with public education dollars, perhaps with supplements from the parents, but are allowed to be run by parent councils without interference from public education authorities.

As with the private schools, problems with charter schools arise when children are forced into the mold of the charter school but do not fit there. The charter policies for these schools state that despite the focus of the school, all children must be eligible to attend. This allows ambitious parents to enroll their children regardless of whether they fit the intent of that school's focus. Many kids, for example, might not have the necessary aptitude for science, but find themselves enrolled in the school anyway. Particular problems are experienced both in private and charter schools by children with learning disabilities or Attention Deficit

Disorder, as these schools generally have no special education facilities for them.

For parents who choose to keep their children in the public education system but are nevertheless still ambitious, enrichment programs, such as bilingual schools and those offering the International Baccalaureate (IB) or Advanced Placement (AP) programs, become popular. Bilingual schools are especially important to Canadian parents as the country is officially bilingual and many careers are enhanced by the ability to speak French. Unfortunately, not all students have an "ear" for languages and are stressed by trying to function in two languages when they only live in one. The IB and AP programs are highly enriched academic programs where students do university-level work and obtain credit for it by the time they are in Grade 12. Schools compete to offer these programs because of the superior students they tend to draw. Unfortunately, these programs are also not for everyone. Those with borderline ability levels, who have achieved the minimum qualifying standards through hard work, struggle to keep up in these courses and often eventually drop out due to the complex course content and heavy homework load. The stress that results from doing poorly in these highly enriched courses can cause depression and lowered self-esteem in students who would have done well in the regular program.

> "It's such a tragedy. Adults have lost touch with the basic needs of the child. It's parenting as product development. Everything about children's lives these days seems to be so serious, and play looks like it is not valuable enough....I just don't think parents – or even policy makers – understand that children's spontaneous, self-generated play has tremendous potential to actually enhance brain development and increase kids' intelligence and academic ability."
>
> **Dr. Jane Healy, author of *Endangered Minds: Why Children Don't Think And What We Can Do About It* (1999) quoted in the *Pittsburgh Post-Gazette***

The movement by parents to get the best possible education for their child so that they can have a greater chance of succeeding in the career world has too many dangers to be entered into blindly. Before parents seek to enrich their children's education beyond that provided in the Kindergarten to Grade 12 public system, they must know whether the child can benefit from this enrichment. A few can but most will not. Parents should let their children develop naturally and enjoy their educational experience, rather than push them to develop too early and farther than they can actually progress. Certainly if the child experiences educational problems, or genuinely finds school not challenging enough, then a thorough psycho-educational assessment should be undertaken by a qualified psychologist to determine the nature of the problem and a solution to it. If they are flourishing in their environment, however, then parents should leave their education to the educators to avoid the many stressors that pushing too hard can create.

## The Pressure for Post-Secondary Education

Of course, the development of a child "product" does not stop with graduation from high school. To the contrary, most modern parents see a child who does not continue her studies beyond Grade 12 as a failure. As a result, the pressure for post-secondary education, the need to get the high grades required to get accepted into college or university, is yet another source of stress that parents place on their children.

While this post-secondary pressure has been present for many years, it has intensified greatly in recent years. Where once the police force required only a Grade 10 education for its recruits, a college diploma is now the minimum requirement. In the 1970s, all one needed to be a chartered accountant was a high school diploma plus a three-year apprenticeship. Today a university degree is necessary. Even the armed forces, which once only asked for a high school education to be an officer, now require a university degree for most of its branches. Statistics Canada estimates two-thirds of new jobs created in Canada by 2008 will require post-secondary education. Certainly, to enter into any profession, which brings with it the higher salaries and benefits that most people now expect, one needs post-secondary education.

The demand for better-educated employees has resulted in enormous enrollment pressures on colleges and universities. For years these institutions have been constantly expanding, but still the pressure for student places has continued. The inevitable byproduct of this enrollment pressure has been the gradual raising of the marks required for acceptance. As the marks have risen, so too has the stress on students to obtain high marks in secondary school. As the educational systems in Canada and the U.S. are somewhat different, each will be examined separately.

In Canada there are two major forms of post-secondary education, college and university. Colleges programs generally take two or three years and culminate in the awarding of a diploma. Generally the academic standards to attend these institutions are lower than those of universities, but that is not necessarily the case for some of the more popular courses. Universities grant degrees, including the Bachelor of Arts or Bachelor of Science degrees, and also include the professional faculties such as Law and Medicine. Over the past decade entrance requirements for both types of post-secondary institutions have gradually crept higher so that in 2003 the entrance standards, averaged across faculties, for the top 15 Canadian Universities were as follows:

| University | Entrance Mark Required | University | Entrance Mark Required |
|---|---|---|---|
| Montreal | 87.9% | Western Ontario | 84% |
| British Columbia | 87.7% | Dalhousie | 83.9% |
| Queen's | 87.5% | Alberta | 83.4% |
| Toronto | 85.9% | Ottawa | 82.4% |
| Laval | 85.3% | Calgary | 82% |
| McGill | 85.3% | McMaster | 81.2% |
| Saskatchewan | 85% | Manitoba | 80.5% |
| Sherbrooke | 84.5% | | |

These standards are extremely high and mean that, of the 77 percent of students who graduate from a Canadian high school, only about 24 percent are able to meet the standards to attend a university. Another 28 percent of high school graduates qualify for college entrance. This means that, while these students will more than likely be able to obtain good jobs, they are excluded from the high-profile careers such as doctor, lawyer, accountant, or engineer, unless they follow their college diploma with the necessary university program.

In the United States there is a greater number and diversity of post-secondary schools, but the main standard is the four-year college program (roughly equivalent to that offered by Canadian universities). In America, according to a 2003 report by the Manhattan Institute, about 70 percent of students in public high schools obtain high school diplomas, but only 32 percent of these students leave high school qualified to attend a four-year college. These figures are for white Americans only. The figures for African-American and Hispanic students are worse. Also, the American population is much more aware of the differences in prestige of the many institutions than are Canadians, with the result that such high-profile schools as Harvard, Yale and Princeton require much higher academic standards than do some of the smaller regional colleges. Competition to get into these schools is fierce, as

## A Disturbing Research Finding

A highly publicized study reported in the journal *Child Development* in 2002 showed that affluent suburban girls in the sixth and seventh grades had higher than expected levels of depression, and that there was high drug and alcohol use among both males and females. The authors partly attributed this stress to excessive achievement pressures. They found that in upwardly mobile suburban communities there was a strong emphasis on ensuring that children secured admission to "stellar colleges." As a result many of these relatively young children felt highly driven to excel not only in academics but at multiple extracurricular activities.

12,000 students apply for every 1000 admissions. The result is that not only are high marks required, but also high Scholastic Aptitude Test Scores and successful participation in extracurricular activities.

The above figures clearly indicate that only a fraction of those who graduate from high school are qualified to attend a university or four-year college. Despite these low numbers, parents place enormous pressure on their children to qualify for these post-secondary programs. After all, as we discussed in the previous section, many parents have been planning for their child's university acceptance since their children were toddlers (or younger). Elementary school teachers now give homework as early as kindergarten to prepare their students for high school and beyond. By the time students begin high school, homework loads can be massive. Teachers and counselors generally start the pressure to reach post-secondary standards in the students' freshman high school year, which might include comments in class and career-track courses. These educators do not intend their comments and programs as pressure, but given that they make students aware of the relative few who will obtain university or college placement, the result is just that.

As evidence of the parental pressure that today's youth feel, the following essay appeared in a high school newspaper in Massachusetts:

**The Speed Of Life**   By Shannon Heneghan

Past generations had some tacky, bizarre ideas. Have you ever looked through your parent's old photo albums and seen ugly vinyl couches, tapered pants, and housewives vacuuming in high heels and pearls? In spite of some frightening interpretations of "style," some good ideas came out of the 50's, 60's, 70's. Families ate meals together. Students left for school in the morning after sunrise. Life was a little more relaxed, a little more reasonable.

Now people live their lives as if they are running a marathon. Everything is a race, from making it to school on time, finishing homework before lunch is over, eating in the 15 minutes between track and drama, and finishing homework before the sun rises and it's time to run the race again. We never even get a water break

Many students leave for school before seven in the morning and do not return home until well after seven in the evening. Some are awake at dawn attending early morning practices, or returning from meets and performances after 10 at night. A package of poptarts from a vending machine constitutes dinner. A good night's rest is unheard of; we fall asleep with our heads in our books. Families rarely see each other long enough to say hello. Our shoulders become tensed up to our ears, our eyes are bloodshot. We just want to call it quits and sleep until July.

The older we get, the faster life's stopwatch seems to tick. We're running out of time to become the state's fastest swimmer, the district's best musician, the nation's best photographer. Anything less than an "A" means we're stupid and we will never go to a good college. If we do not go to Princeton, we will never find a successful career. We'll be poor, living on the streets, starving. We will be complete failures! Whoa! Slow down. We're working so hard, but we never stop and ask ourselves, "What are we working towards?"

Our parents did not worry about college when they were in the seventh grade. Most never stayed up all night studying when they were 12. They were not expected to be the next Mia Hamm or Michael Jordan of the recreational sports teams, or the Yo-Yo Ma of their fifth grade orchestra. They did not experience that kind of extreme pressure until they were in college. We have been stressed to the max since we were just tots.

The next time you are home for more than five minutes, ask your parents what life was like when they were your age (unless you hear, "When I was your age" too much already). Most did not take seven Advanced Placement classes a year. They attended study halls, open campuses, and longer lunches. They ate dinner at home with their families, or they at least saw them more than once a week. They slept more than four hours a night. Some might even say they enjoyed their high school years.

Some of these pressures are the result of a changing society. Though we cannot change increasing school hours, college competition and parents' expectations, we can control how we react to these burdens.

An important lesson has been lost that no book can ever teach, and no MCAS can ever test. Life is not about being smart, the fastest, the most talented. It's not about the colleges we attend, the jobs we hold, the money we make. The truly important things in life are the ones most often forgotten: our families, our friends, a love for what we do. We need to relax and take a good look at the path we tread. Maybe we could even slow to a jog. There's no finish line to cross and no race to win. We do not always even have to run our best times.

Reprinted from *The American Catholic* (January-February, 2003)

## Sports and Extracurricular Activities

In today's educational equations, academics alone will not guarantee results at the university level. There is an expectation that students participate—and succeed at—sports *and* extracurricular activities as well. As a result, parents are pushing their children into a wide range of activities to ensure that these products are as "well rounded" as they can be.

The true purpose of sports and other extracurricular activities in schools is found in the ancient Latin expression *"mens sana in corpore sano"* or, a healthy mind in a healthy body. The fact is that sports are fun for athletically inclined youngsters and, if treated as enjoyable additions to their education, and not as the main purpose of it, sports can be a major incentive to attend school. No matter how interesting the classes are, school sports are usually more enjoyable and give youngsters something to look forward to at the end of each day. The same can be said for everything from school plays to the cheerleading squad. They help to make school more interesting and the student well rounded. Extracurricular activities are not the main reason that students attend school. Similarly sports and other activities unconnected to schools, such as Little League baseball or minor league hockey, are mainly there for enjoyment, exercise, and the learning of new skills.

Extracurricular activities, and sports in particular, have another benefit: competition. Although many concerned parents and educators are against competition in any form, some competitiveness is good for most young people. The best tends to come out in competition and, after all, it is the root of our capitalistic economic system. Problems only appear when children are pushed to produce more than they are capable of, or when more emphasis than should is placed on the activity. Parents, coaches, and teachers need to be realistic when it comes to a youngster's abilities. The coach's job is to teach and motivate while the parents just need to be supportive of both the coach and their youngster. If they can do this, then their children's talent will come through and, if capable of professional sports, the professional theatre or even of being a concert musician, children will make it on the basis of their own talent and determination. Pushing kids beyond their limits or criticizing coaches and teachers for their inability to get the best from their child only adds to the stress on the youngster.

The main source for these problems is the salaries now being paid to professional athletes and entertainers. The fame and incredibly inflated incomes that come with success in these areas become a major lure for young students and even worse, for their parents. All parents want their children to be successful and when they see that their child has some athletic skill, musical talent, or dramatic ability, dreams of vicarious fame and fortune begin. The drive for sports achievement can put incredible stress on all but the most gifted athlete because parental focus is on success in these areas rather than on enjoyment of the activity. The combination of long practices, late weeknight games, pressure to make the team or the starting lineup, and parental pressure to star can be very hard on many young students. On a smaller scale parents can attempt to propel their child to fame in the school dramatic or musical production or try to make their daughters into fashion models.

We have all heard of horror stories of "hockey dads" who are obsessed with their child's potential success on the rink, or the "stage mom" who fantasizes that her daughter will become a Hollywood starlet. To be sure, most parents do not become obsessive about their children's athletic or entertainment potential. But even "mild mannered" parents, knowing that extracurricular success can play a major role in university acceptance, can place pressures on their children to perform. The result is that activities designed to add fun and excitement to a child's life, both in school and out, as well as to teach such concepts as teamwork and sportsmanship, creates stress and bitterness within the family and a total loss of interest in an activity the child once enjoyed.

# Teach Your Children

As parents have become so caught up in seeing education as the primary means for developing and marketing their "product" children, they have forgotten a crucial aspect in education: the teaching of values. Parents simply do not actively teach their children the basic principles of life that will help them to live happily and prevent them from harm. These are values such as honesty, courage, self-discipline, moderation, loyalty, respect, love, kindness, and unselfishness. It seems incredible that parents could overlook a task that has been one of their major responsibilities throughout history, yet this is indeed occurring. What happens when parents abandon this crucial educational role?

Front-page news stories for the past several years about teenage sex and violence have continually shocked and horrified readers. These stories, which included school shootings in Springfield, Oregon; Jonesboro, Arkansas; West Paducah, Kentucky; and Pearl, Mississippi, climaxed with the almost unbelievable events at Columbine High School in 1999. There Eric Harris and Dylan Klebold killed 12 students and a teacher. While the events were covered in great detail in the news media, little was reported about the families of the young people involved. Investigators found that Harris and Klebold had been planning the event for almost two years, yet the parents apparently knew nothing about it. This appears to be the epitome of parents who were not involved enough with their children and who did not effectively teaching them right from wrong.

A more widespread example of media evidence of the lack of value teaching to children was shown in a 1999 episode of the PBS series *Frontline*. "The Lost Children of Rockdale County" detailed the incredible sexual escapades of about 200 teenagers in a suburban community about 25 miles east of Atlanta. These teens, some as young as 13, were engaging in a wide variety of promiscuous sexual practices, including oral, anal, and group sex;

some girls had sexual histories that included up to 100 partners. The reason the community came to official attention was a major outbreak of syphilis, a sexually transmitted disease rarely occuring in affluent areas. In all, over 200 teens were treated for this disease. The investigator, Dr. Claire Sterk of Emory University in Atlanta, concluded:

> If there was one common element, it wasn't being a single parent because some [kids] had both parents and some had older siblings as role models. The one common element was that the parents all wanted the best for their kid—the best often meaning material stuff. Many worked long hours and emphasized the "stuff" they could afford to give their kids—a TV, an audio system. But what the alienated and struggling kids wanted was attention, somebody to relate to, *somebody who can step in and provide guidance*. (italics mine)

In other words, no adults were spending time with these teens to help them to deal with the peer pressure that developed in their community. No one was actively teaching about the proper place of sex in society. The result? The adolescents just went with their own emotions, with rather disastrous personal and public health consequences.

More scientific research has also confirmed the absence of values teaching. In 2000, the YMCA in the United States released a study about principal issues facing the average modern family. The survey found that 44 percent of respondents cited a "lack of morals and values education" in families. Another 60 percent of adults thought that communication between parents and children has worsened over the previous decade, and 62 percent believed that parents needed to devote more time to their children. The impact of this parental neglect was clear to the researchers. "Despite a booming economy," they wrote, "many parents are working more hours, trying to make ends meet. This leaves millions of young people spending vulnerable hours unsupervised: susceptible to isolation, peer pressure, and risk behaviors."

Parents are spending less time with their children and even in the diminished time they do spend together, they are not teaching their children values to live by. Children are then left to make their own decisions on moral matters, putting them under tremendous stress and even danger. Children, even older teenagers, do not want to make all their own decisions. They need a set of guidelines to work within to feel safe and secure. These guidelines are normally provided by a disciplinary structure within the home and by parents and educators giving them a set of moral guidelines to follow. Lacking other reference points when faced with a moral dilemma such as whether to use drugs, have sex, steal, or vandalize, they often turn to their peers and the media for guidance. Unfortunately friends lack the maturity to make prudent decisions in moral areas and the media, through films, television, and glossy magazines are severely blurring sound morals and values, especially in the areas of sex and violence. The inevitable result is that the behavior of today's generation of children often reflects these blurred guidelines. They are not sure what is best for them so they do what feels best. This is not an acceptable situation.

## What Happened to Morality?

The question as to why parents are often not teaching their children morals and values is a complex one. It may have started with the relatively recent movement away from organized religion. Until the 1950s, family attendance at church on Sunday's was a common occurrence. Most families participated in organized religion of some kind. Here moral values, as exemplified by the Ten Commandments, were preached and taught. Children not only learned these values in Sunday School, but had them reinforced by their parents at home throughout the week. Organized religion provided a clear set of values for everyone to follow. From these original values, laws were made that developed these values into common core beliefs of society as a whole, regardless of whether or not they practiced any specific religion. These included laws against theft, violence and even marital practices.

Unfortunately, probably due to the failure of the religious institutions to move with the times, church attendance began to fall off in the 1960s and has continued to do so ever since. For example, according to the Barna Research Group, a California-based organization that provides information and analysis regarding cultural trends and the Christian Church, average church attendance has fallen from 102 persons per service in 1992 to 90 in 1999. It is probably accurate to state that today the majority of families do not attend church. This then removes the foundation of fundamental values from their lives and, unless replaced with some other moral code, leaves parents floundering. They aren't passing on a coherent set of rules of conduct to their children, because they don't have one themselves.

Certainly religion is not yet dead and some of the flourishing ones, such as the Church of Jesus Christ of Latter Day Saints (Mormons) and many evangelical churches, are very effectively teaching morals and values. Unfortunately these groups are now in the minority, with most people choosing not to follow a structured religion.

The major difficulty for parents appears to be that they themselves are struggling with what they believe in. For example, many have some experience of drugs from their youth, and they are confused as to what to tell their children about them. They know that the children should not be using them, but they are conflicted as to how to communicate this without sounding hypocritical. It is the same for sex. Parents lack the knowledge about what to tell their children about proper sexual behavior, and even if they know what to tell them, they lack the conviction and confidence to have frank conversations. In the church-going days the rule was clear—no sex before marriage. While this rule was often broken, it generally caused young people to hold off their sexual behavior until much later in their lives, often until they were at least in love. Now parental confusion is causing many parents to say nothing at all, leaving the children to set their own guidelines. Without clear ideas on what they believe in, parents cannot give their children a set of guidelines that will help them control their lives and avoid conflict and heartache.

Another problem for parents is that many are of the opinion that they should not be telling their children how to think and act. Perhaps as an outgrowth of some of the hippie philosophies of the 1960s and 1970s, many adults actually believe that they should let their children develop their own ideas of how to act. They feel that it is dictatorial and conformist for them to impose their concepts on their children. This distorted thinking again leaves these children in a moral vacuum that forces them to develop their own, often erroneous, codes of conduct.

If parents want to convey a clear set of guidelines for moral behavior, they need to set the example for their children. If you do not want your children to smoke or use alcohol, then don't smoke or drink alcohol yourself. Certainly if you do not want your children to use drugs, then you cannot either. Bringing home office supplies from work for personal use teaches them that stealing is all right, and swearing at other drivers on the freeway encourages the use of foul language among the younger members of the family. In this regard parents should not think that they can hide these behaviors from the kids. They will know no matter how hard you try to cover up. Children want to look up to their parents as responsible adults. They do not want to see them acting immorally or illegally. They need them to set the example so that they know how they should act.

Finally, there is the problem of time. Once again the recent trend towards working harder and longer, by both parents, is causing problems for the youngsters. Having less time to spend with the children is resulting in less communication within the family. Family dinners, a traditional time of catching up on the day's activities, have become a rarity in many homes. Weekends are usually taken up with catching up on the household chores that have been neglected all week. Many fathers still believe that they should have some leisure activities, such as playing golf or watching sports. The combination of these factors makes the time available for talking to the children very limited indeed.

The problem is that when parents aren't communicating frequently with their children, they don't know what is going on in their lives. For example, a normal conversation after a teenager returns from a party might elicit the information that alcohol was present. This would be a perfect time to begin a discussion about how the teenager feels about drinking and for the parent to put in their commercial about how they don't want their children using alcohol. Similarly, while watching a relatively explicit sexual scene together in a TV show or movie, parents have the perfect opportunity to ask their child how he or she feels about sexual intercourse and when they think it should begin. They can then slip in their ideas so that the youngster has a clear idea of what the parents believe in. Parents have to be together with their children when these "teachable moments" occur so that they can use them to convey their morals and values.

The shift of today's society away from giving the family the highest value is resulting in stress and confusion in our children. While the women's movement has addressed some basic injustices of modern culture it has created others. Even though the demands of the workplace have increased in many businesses, the veneration of a strong work ethic is going far beyond what most jobs require. Similarly, while it is nice to have a huge house with several cars in the garage and TVs in every room, these are not only not necessary to the raising of emotionally healthy children, but are becoming a detriment since parents are busier earning money than they are with raising their children. Finally, children need to know right from wrong and the unwillingness of many parents to value values themselves is stressful and confusing to kids.

Two major education-related factors appear to be at work that are putting too much pressure on children. One is the push to get their children ahead of the game by starting their education as soon as possible, then pushing the children hard all the way through the grades. While parents need to be aware of what their children are doing in school and need to ensure that the kids are doing as well as possible, too often they are going too far and placing too much emphasis on the educational process.

The other educational factor causing stress to children is the failure of parents to actively teach their children morals and values. Without these guiding principles, children are left to make their own decisions on right and wrong, without the maturity to

### Teaching Values to Your Children

The best ways for a parent to teach values are:

- Know your own values. If you yourself are confused, you will pass on the confusion to your children.

- Practice what you preach. Children are sponges and they will learn to apply and live the values they are taught only if they see you doing the same.

- Articulate your values clearly and simply.

- Explain to your child why you hold those particular values rather than any others.

- Accept that your child will add her own unique interpretation to the values you teach.

- Make sure that practice of those values by your child is acknowledged, praised and encouraged e.g. telling the truth about a misdeed may be treated as commuting a part of the offence.

Source: www.indianmoms.com

do this effectively. Often they make the wrong decisions, then find themselves in trouble. Parents must make the teaching of morality a priority if they are to help their children live wholesome lives without the stress of making their own difficult decisions.

# CHAPTER VI

# Discipline

**A**s the previous chapter made clear, parents are unwilling or unable to transmit their own values to their children. Closely related to this is parental confusion about disciplinary techniques. When parents do not know when or how to discipline their children, they usually end up doing it poorly. The result is that young people do not know where their boundaries lie and may even wonder whether their parents really care about them.

The impact of an absence of discipline is most obviously felt in the home environment. Undisciplined children will often come and go when they please, steal from their parents and siblings and drink or use drugs frequently. The combination of weak or non-existent family discipline and the desire for freedom and independence that develops in adolescents can become an unmanageable and even dangerous situation.

The inability of poorly disciplined young people to make sound moral decisions often results in criminal acts such as shoplifting, vandalism, and even violence. Although youth crime rates have been declining since the early 1990s, they still remain unacceptably high in Canada and the United States. Many cities in both countries have become so worried about these crime rates that they have imposed nighttime curfews on the youth in their jurisdictions. A 2000 survey by the National League of Cities indicated that almost

70 percent of the 490 American cities polled had nighttime youth curfews, while about 14 percent even had daytime curfews (where youth under 18 must not be on the streets during school hours). Bob Knight, the league president, commented that curfews "continue to be a growing trend in the United States as city officials look for answers to ensure the safety of youth in their communities." Canadian cities and towns, such as Red Deer, Alberta, and Huntington, Quebec, have adopted similar curfews. While the effectiveness of these curfews can be debated, the very fact that municipal authorities believe they are necessary indicates that too many parents are not doing their job when it comes to maintaining control of their children.

Parents certainly do not want to find themselves in situations where their children are running the household and possibly engaging in criminal behavior. The problem is that over the past few decades the entire sphere of disciplining children has become so confused that many parents do not understand how to discipline their children, and some do not even understand why it is necessary.

## The Purpose of Discipline

Discipline is often considered a punitive process, but its major purpose is to teach young children how to conduct themselves in ways considered by society to be acceptable, without adult supervision. It is the process of taking an infant, who is totally dependent on adults, and assisting the child to become a self-sufficient and independent adult. Discipline builds self-esteem and positive relationships between adults and children. It teaches responsibility, respect for self and others, problem-solving skills, self-control, and independent thinking. Few parents should disagree with the importance of these skills.

Discipline, then, is mainly about teaching decision-making. It teaches children how to make better choices about their behavior and how to be responsible. It shows them that they have the power to choose how they act and behave. Many parents, however, are confused about the purpose of discipline. Some believe that it is about controlling their child's behavior, so that their emphasis is on making the child behave in all circumstances. To achieve this control, they may use punitive measures and anger, creating tension and indecision in their child. Other parents believe that, because to discipline is to control, the use of punitive measures will damage their child's self-esteem, so they do not set any disciplinary standards at all. While both approaches are ineffective, the latter one is perhaps the worst approach of all.

Children whose parents either do not believe in discipline or use ineffective disciplinary techniques may become selfish, greedy, dishonest, uncooperative, and insecure. These youngsters are often disrespectful to others and they can be destructive and aggressive. In fact, they can become all the things that municipal authorities

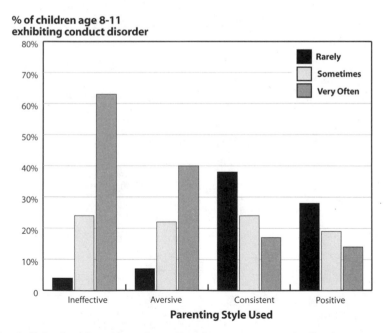

Fig. 6: Behavioural problems increase when parents use ineffective parenting styles — Statistics Canada, 1994 and 1995 National Longitudinal Survey of Children and Youths, Cycles 1 & 2

worry about when they are forced to set youth curfews. An excellent 2001 report from the Canadian Centre for Justice Statistics clearly showed how behavioral problems increased when poor disciplinary parenting styles are employed (see Fig. 6). It is fascinating to note that more behavioral problems were noted with ineffective disciplinary techniques (basically little or no discipline at all) than there were with harsh punitive ones. Even so, much more positive results were obtained by using a consistent disciplinary style and even better results with a positive or teaching approach. These various techniques will be discussed in detail in a later section.

An excellent summary of why children need discipline has been published by the U.S. National Parent Teacher Association. This organization agrees that disciplining children is a teaching process that should be a positive way of helping and guiding children. Specifically, discipline has the following benefits:

- **For protection**. Parents need to discipline very young children to protect them from such dangers as street traffic, hot stoves, or electrical outlets.

- **To get along with others**. Discipline helps children learn to socialize effectively with others and to develop self-control so as to avoid interpersonal conflict.

- **To understand limits**. Discipline teaches children acceptable behavior, such as not taking other children's property, hitting them, or breaking things in anger.

To this list should be added that discipline helps children to feel safe and secure as they know where their boundaries are and realize that their parents are there to care for them and protect them. This security helps to build children's self-confidence by giving them a safe and caring environment from which to learn new skills and social behaviors.

In maintaining an effective system of discipline, parents help children to think and act in an orderly manner, to understand the consequences of their actions, and to learn the values that are held by their family and community. These seem like goals that any parent would want to set for their children. The question is: Why are so many parents failing to use effective discipline on their children?

## What Happened to Discipline?

To understand what has happened to family discipline, we need a brief review of the history of families and child rearing in North America.

The original European settlers who came to the United States were freedom-minded individuals wanting to be rid of the oppression of the European noble classes. Many wanted religious freedom from state-mandated churches, but others sought economic freedom and, with it, the opportunity to earn a decent living and have some control over their own futures.

The desire for religious freedom by the Puritans, combined with their Calvinistic work ethic and desire for land of their own, led to the development of an entrepreneurial society that highly valued personal freedom and independence. This desire eventually led them to throw off the yoke of British rule and to establish their own country, with a government based less on the whims of a monarch and more on the will of the majority.

The French settlers of Canada were less concerned with religious freedom than they were with having their own land or being able to make a good living from farming or the fur trade. After the English conquered Quebec in 1759, little initially changed until the arrival of another group seeking freedom—the United Empire Loyalists. This group was composed of independent-thinking people who wished to remain associated with England, as opposed to their fellow Americans who wanted political freedom from the British king.

What was common to all these groups was their desire for personal freedom and their contempt for tyrannical rule. This contempt very quickly spread to their parenting practices. Kay Hymowitz explained this development: "In the early days of the republic, Americans overthrew the harsh Calvinist discipline founded on fear and absolute obedience to introduce a new child-rearing that appealed to children's affections and emerging reason that the young democracy required a new man, independent and self-governing."

It is doubtful that American or Canadian mothers and fathers sat down and decided that they needed to modify their parenting practices to produce the independent thinkers required by their new democracies. More likely the new parenting practices arose gradually from the type of people who had the courage and foresight to leave their familiar surroundings for the unknown rigors of the New World. These were independent-minded pioneers who valued individual freedoms and applied these values to their parenting. The result was disciplinary practices that allowed children to make choices, albeit somewhat limited in scope, rather than forcing them to do the parent's bidding.

Over a century after the founding of the United States, this parenting philosophy was articulated in H. Clay Trumbull's *Hints on Child Training*, published in 1891. Trumbull explained that "will-training is an important element in child-training; but will-breaking has no part or place in the training of a child." Trumbull elaborated, noting that "a broken will is worth as much in its sphere as a broken bow; just that, and no more. A child with a broken will is not so well furnished for the struggle of life as a child with only one arm, or one leg, or one eye. Such a child has no power of strong personality, or of high achievement in the world."

By "will-training," Trumbull sought to expand the child's "faculty of choosing or deciding between two courses of action." To illustrate his point, Trumbull used the example of a child who refuses to close the door.

Most readers, and indeed even the most liberal of modern parenting authorities, would have been delighted with the Rev.

Trumbull's initial suggestion of keeping anger out of the situation: "Let the parent turn to the child in loving gentleness,—not then in severity, and never, never, never in anger,—and tell him tenderly of a better way than that which he is pursuing, urging him to a wiser nobler choice. When the child refuses to make the "nobler choice," Turnbull suggests another route: "Let the parent say to the child: 'Johnny, I shall give you a choice in this matter. You can either shut the door or take a whipping.' Then a new choice is before the boy, and his will is free and unbroken for its meeting." Unfortunately, the choice itself—obey or receive a whipping—was the main reason that parenting philosophy began to move past the earlier democratic thought to an even more liberal position. By the middle of the twentieth century, the use of corporal punishment in discipline began to be questioned as potentially abusive and traumatic. As well, it began to be seen as having the possibility of conditioning violence with consequences, teaching children themselves to respond to frustration physically. Much to Trumbull's disappointment (had he been around), "whipping" was going out of style.

Some of the early responsibility for the questioning of corporal punishment as a disciplinary tool can be laid at the feet of the modern founder of the study of the mind, Sigmund Freud. By emphasizing the drastic consequences of an unhappy childhood, he introduced guilt into the framework of parenting. Gradually parenting authorities started to question the value of corporal punishment because they linked it with traumatizing the young child. Horrified at the possibility of psychological damage to children, parenting experts began to preach the merits of discipline without corporal punishment. Consider, for example, the views from 1940 of Professor C.W. Valentine of the University of Birmingham. Valentine taught the writings of Freud, and was one of the early authorities to question the value of corporal punishment, and indeed, any punishment for children at all. In *The Difficult Child and the Problem of Discipline*, he wrote that the term 'discipline' was "far from being identical with punishment and still further from corporal punishment. Though penalties may be necessary at times, both parent and teacher can 'keep good discipline' with very little, or even no, punishment so far as the majority of children are concerned."

Statements such as these from noted people in the child-raising field began to sow confusion in the minds of parents. These authorities were beginning to say what not to do, but they were not saying what parents should do. Nowhere in his book does Professor Valentine say what disciplinary practices should replace corporal punishment. Even worse, how are parents to discipline their children with no punishments at all? Few prescriptions are given.

By the 1950s views about discipline had progressed from corporal punishment being a standard disciplinary consequence to spankings being allowed only infrequently. The problem was when to spank and when not to. And if you don't spank, what should you do? Some recent writers, including Kay Hymowitz, have unfairly blamed this confusion on Dr. Benjamin Spock, who wrote *Baby and Child Care* in 1946. Although he certainly contributed to it, the trend away from corporal punishment had already started, and Spock was merely parroting other writers in his advice to new parents. In fact, on the subject of spanking, he initially felt it had some value. In the original edition of his book he wrote: "I'm not particularly advocating spanking, but I think it's less poisonous than lengthy disapproval, because it clears the air for parent and child. You sometimes hear it recommended that you never spank a child in anger but wait until you have cooled off. That seems unnatural. It takes a pretty grim parent to whip a child when the anger is gone."

There are good reasons that Dr. Spock's book has become one of the biggest sellers of all time. One of them may be the relaxed, positive approach he stresses for dealing with young children. He appears to be trying to take the fear out of parenting infants, and he does this very well. Unfortunately, a by-product of this approach may have spilled over into the disciplinary area, lulling parents into thinking that kids should discipline themselves naturally, just as they should eat, sleep, and take the pacifier when they want to. However, a careful reading of Spock's section on discipline shows that he did advocate firmness in discipline. But he did not like to emphasize its punishment aspects. In this he is absolutely right, but somehow his message of firmness with a minimal use of punishment got lost.

The result of the movement against punishing children was a general confusion among parents about how to discipline their children. While there was no shortage of parenting books around saying what not to do, most were very vague on exactly what parents should do when their child misbehaved. In his best-selling 1965 book, *Between Parent & Child*, Dr. Haim Ginott framed the problem: "What is the difference between the approach of our grandparents and of ourselves in disciplining children? What grandfather did was done with authority; whatever we do is done with hesitation. Even when in error, grandfather acted with certainty. Even when in the right, we act with doubt."

The problem was that when you took away the immediacy and simplicity of a spanking, or even of sending a child to his or her room, you needed to replace it with something much more complex. What was required was to be able to engage the child in a learning dialogue that would indicate that the action was inappropriate and what the appropriate action would be—while having the child feel good about this learning experience and not repeating the same action. This complex dialogue is extremely difficult to come up with on the spot. In fact, it is so difficult that most parents found it too hard to understand. They knew that they shouldn't spank or even punish, but what they should do was all too vague. Ginott's explanation of this new approach provides a classic example of this complexity. "The modern approach helps the child both with his feelings and conduct. The parents allow the child to speak out about what he feels, but limit and direct undesirable acts. The limits are set in a manner that preserves the self-respect of the parent as well as the child. The limits are neither arbitrary nor capricious, but educational and character-building."

Perfectly clear? Your child has just hit a friend over the head with a toy truck and you have to think of how to get him not to do that again without using punishment, but also in a way that preserves everyone's self-respect and is educational and character-building. Is it any wonder parents were baffled? Worse, many became paralyzed. Parents became so fearful of crippling their children psychologically by restraining their natural and creative instincts that they allowed their family discipline to erode.

The status of family discipline continued to drift along in relative limbo until a new movement in the 1980s added even more confusion. The buzz-word of that decade was "self-esteem," and its development in young children became the focus of child-raising experts. To develop this self-esteem, parents needed to use natural and logical consequences when they disciplined their children. Any attempts to control their behavior would be damaging and therefore should be avoided. Neither rewards nor punishments should be used in this approach because they were deemed to be based on external controls, while what parents needed to do was develop their child's inner controls. Punishments were seen as attempts to hurt children, whether physically, mentally, or emotionally, in order to teach them a lesson. Rewards were seen as bribery, which failed to instill self-confidence.

This movement was really an extension of Freudian "guilt" theory. Not only would parents avoid traumatizing their children by punishing them, but they would also build self-esteem by allowing their children to experience logical and natural consequences for their behavior. The cornerstones of this approach were threefold: (1) children are responsible for their own behavior; (2) they are allowed to make their own decisions and to learn from their successes and their mistakes; and (3) children learn from the reality of the natural and social order rather than from forced compliance to the wishes of authority figures.

Laudatory as these cornerstones are, the whole approach of logical and natural consequences was far too subject to misinterpretation. It was difficult for parents to tell when they should or should not act. Consider the following statement of Dr. Louise Hart, one of the proponents of this movement: "Parents must realize that every kid is frisky and mischievous at times. It is how they express their individuality and aliveness. If they want to do something and it doesn't hurt them, let them do it. Give in on the little things"

Using this approach, if your children are running wild in a restaurant, you should not do anything because their actions are not harmful to themselves; they are merely being "frisky and mischievous." It is doubtful that Dr. Hart actually intended this interpretation, but her statement illustrates just how open this approach is to misunderstanding.

The self-esteem approach to discipline is also difficult to apply because finding natural and logical consequences is not always easy. Certainly if your child oversleeps, as is the case in one of Dr. Hart's examples, then it is logical to allow the child to be late for school as a natural consequence. But what if the child doesn't mind being late? How far do you let this natural cycle flow before parental intervention is necessary? There are many other instances where natural consequences do not easily come to mind. What do you do if your 15-year-old son takes the family car for a joy ride? Do you allow him to keep doing it until he gets caught by the police or has an accident? How much self-esteem should a parent build before the child is completely out of control?

The result of the movement to build self-esteem was to add further confusion to a subject that had already been increasingly muddled over the past 60 years. Unfortunately the muddling did not stop with the 1980s. In fact, it is still going on.

In 2003 researchers at the University of Guelph observed the verbal and non-verbal responses of children to parental requests in 40 families. The requests were relatively simple, such as "Clean up your room" or "Pick up your toys." The study found that the kids listened to about one-third of their parents' requests, and during the times that kids were listening, parents got what they wanted about half the time. More worrisome was the fact that 17 percent of the children who did comply set their own terms for compliance. When the researchers broke down all the results statistically, they showed that parents received what they wanted from their children in less than 1 of 6 cases, and even then some had to negotiate to get them to do what they asked.

That finding alone should have been a wake-up call for parents throughout North America because it clearly showed that children were not listening to their parents, and that the parents were apparently helpless to do anything about it. That it was not such a call was likely due to the authors' conclusion that the parent-child negotiations were in fact good for their relationship. Nothing was said about the three-quarters of children who did not comply. The authors actually managed to put a positive spin on a horrible finding, making it seem as if there is nothing wrong with most children not complying with simple parental requests.

It is this kind of information that is so confusing to parents. Parents have begun to believe that discipline is bad for children as a result of this kind of academic research. Modern parents have little time to read parenting books and academic studies as it is, and when they do, they do not need to end up more baffled than when they started. That is precisely what has happened to field of discipline. It has been tinkered with, for the best of reasons, for all too long. The results of poor discipline are now apparent for all to see and a clarification and simplification of the entire process is badly needed.

## The Consequences of Poor Discipline

Most authorities agree that weak or non-existent family discipline results in children with poor decision-making skills, a lack of respect for authority, and unhealthy moral development. While the lack of discipline is not the only contributor, continued high youth crime rates are a major result of the confusion reigning in most of today's families. The statistics are very clear. As indicated by the graphs, the rates of youth crime, particularly violent crime, are still unacceptably high, despite educational programs and improved security measures. Both Canada and the U.S. have lowered the overall youth crime rate since the early 1990s, but it remains a huge problem for parents and law enforcement authorities alike.

Weak or non-existent family discipline does not necessarily produce criminals, but the results can still be very hard on children and

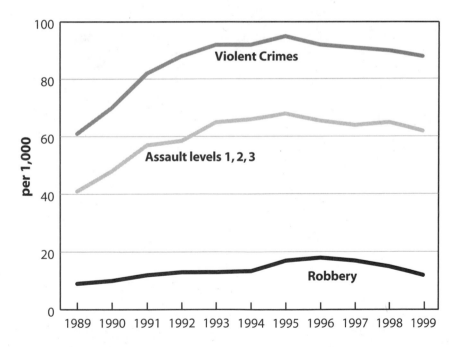

Fig. 4: Youth violent crime in Canada has risen over the past decade, but has stabilized since 1993. **Statistics Canada, Canadian Centre for Justice Statistics, Uniform Crime Reporting Survey.**

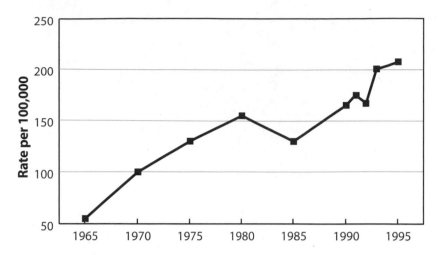

Fig. 5: U.S. Arrest Rates for Violent Crime—Youth Ages 18: 1965–1994
Note: Violent crimes include murder, rape, robbery, and aggravated assault.
Rates refer to the number of arrests made per 100,000 inhabitants belonging
to the prescribed age group. **Source: Uniform Crime Reporting Program, FBI.**

parents. This is particularly true of the present situation in schools, not only in North America, but also throughout the developed world.

## Discipline in the Schools

The confusion today's parents feel about effective disciplinary practices is mirrored in the school system. Reports from many countries recount the same problem: discipline in the schools is a major concern. Consider the following examples:

• In Britain in 2001, the BBC's web site asked, "How can poor discipline in schools in England be reversed?" The web site was flooded with responses from across the country.

• In Canada in 2002, the Alberta Teachers' Association published a report titled *Falling Through the Cracks: A Summary of What We Heard About Teaching and Learning Conditions in Alberta Schools.* The study showed how teachers and school administrators are frustrated with the disciplinary conditions in their schools and how they feel helpless to meet the educational needs of their students given the current disciplinary climate.

• In 2004 in New Zealand, a report by the Maxim Institute indicated that discipline is the primary concern of parents about schooling in that country.

• In 2004 the New York-based Public Agenda for the Common Good surveyed 750 American schools about discipline. The survey found that 85 percent of teachers and 73 percent of parents felt that ineffective school discipline had an impact on student learning. As well, 82 percent of teachers and 74 percent of parents believed that the demise of school discipline stemmed from the failure of parents to teach their children discipline at home.

In this last example, we can assume that most of the parents surveyed were probably referring to other parents and not to themselves, but perhaps many are beginning to realize that they are the root cause of a disciplinary deficit in schools. For years teachers have been bedeviled by a lack of parental support for their disciplinary practices. As recently as the 1960s, students who misbehaved at school could expect equal consequences at home if their parents found out. This is not the case today, and teachers now expect parental wrath and even lawsuits when they discipline a child. Students themselves constantly remind teachers that they have rights and their parents can sue when they are reprimanded.

Since schools are public institutions, they must respond to what that public wants from their education system. Over the past two decades school systems have attempted to give parents more input into education through the creation of parent councils and PTA-style organizations. The idea behind this trend is that greater public input into how schools are run will make them more responsive to our changing society. Unfortunately, the parent councils tend to be mainly fund-raising organizations, with little power to make changes in the school system. Schools are left feeling pressured by aggressive parents to reduce or eliminate the consequences for the misbehavior of their undisciplined children. For some reason, possibly because they are also confused about what constitutes effective discipline, school administrators have listened to these outspoken parents, with the result that discipline in many schools has sunk to alarming levels.

It was not that long ago that coming to school drunk or under the influence of drugs meant instant expulsion. As one Calgary, Alberta, school principal used to say to parents, "Alcohol or drugs on you or in you—you're gone." Today the most that intoxicated students will receive is a two- to five-day suspension. It was the same for physical aggression. Attacking another student or a teacher meant expulsion out of the school system entirely. Now the student may have to leave his or her present school, but the system is obligated to find another school for the aggressor. Such responses have become a trading game among principals: I'll take one of yours if you take one of mine. Given that they rarely face major consequences for what used to be major offences, students now consider that they can do what they want with impunity. The final outcome has become chaos in many classrooms.

Instead of focusing on teaching, many instructors have become forced to concentrate more on keeping order in the classroom. The new battle cry of the acting-out student is "My parents will sue you"—and they do. Without the support of their administrators, teachers can do little about misbehavior if they do not have a forceful personality. If they throw the miscreant out, the student will be back almost immediately, with even less respect for order and discipline. A report by Harvey Rice, a state-appointed safe schools advocate in Philadelphia, explained this situation in 2002. Rice reported that he was "troubled by the School District of

Philadelphia's continued reluctance to punish violent perpetrators and those possessing weapons in school. The continued acceptance of violent and disruptive behavior is totally unacceptable and infringes on the right of every good student in the [district] to get the quality education that he or she is entitled to."

Why was Rice so concerned? During the 2001-2002 school year, the School District of Philadelphia reported 3,690 violent incidents, including assault, assault with a weapon, abduction, arson, robbery, and sexual assault. Of these, only five offenders were expelled from the school district. Another 108 offenders were transferred to disciplinary schools. The remaining 97 percent received a suspension, a lateral transfer to a different school, or no punishment at all.

The situation in Canadian schools is not much different. In 2003 the *Calgary Herald* ran a three-part series of editorials criticizing school authorities for exactly the same things that were occurring in the Philadelphia system. The basic theme was that more teachers were needed because discipline in the classrooms had become a major problem. The second editorial was headlined "Attempts to Discipline Students Hampered by Political Correctness." It very clearly pointed out that much of the problem resulted from a philosophy of discipline that emphasized not traumatizing children, building self-esteem, and avoiding "punishment." But if these school administrators had a more realistic grasp of the purpose of discipline and the most effective ways of maintaining it, they would not cave in to the pressure from aggressive parents, who are desperately trying not to believe that their child could do anything wrong. The irony is that the discipline problems that schools are experiencing stem from discipline problems in the home, which themselves stem from misguided attempts of academics and educators to humanize discipline in the first place.

The book, *Teaching Interrupted*, produced from research from the Public Agenda for Common Good, offered several key suggestions from teachers and parents for how to correct the disciplinary problems in schools. They included:

- Zero-tolerance policies for serious violations, so that offenders are actually expelled from schools and not traded to another one

- Giving principals more authority to handle discipline issues as they see fit

- Establishing alternative schools for chronic offenders

- Holding parents more accountable for their children's behavior

- Limiting lawsuits to serious situations, such as expulsions

- Removing the possibility of monetary awards for parents who sue over disciplinary issues

- Strictly enforcing the little rules, such as talking in class or disturbing neighboring students, so that the right disciplinary tone is created

- Establishing dress codes

- Putting greater emphasis on classroom management skills in teacher education programs

One of the most disturbing school-based impacts of poor home discipline has been the upturn in bullying. Despite considerable attention being given to the problem of bullying since facts have come to light that almost three-quarters of students involved in school shootings had been bullies, the problem continues to grow. A national study of almost 16,000 students in Grades 6 through 10 is among the most recent to document the scope of bullying in American schools. In this study, psychologist Dr. Tonja R. Nansel and colleagues found that 17 percent of students reported having been bullied "sometimes" or more frequently during the school term. About 19 percent reported bullying others "sometimes" or more often. And 6 percent reported both bullying and having been bullied. These are very high figures that do not seem to be dropping. Some schools in the U.S. and Canada have initiated anti-bullying programs, but to date their effects have been minimal.

It seems incredible in this modern age that, despite our wealth of knowledge and research, such an old problem as bullying is increasing rather than decreasing. The present atmosphere has been described by many authors and researchers as a "culture of bullying." This phrase implies that there are factors in our culture that are contributing to this increase. These factors could easily be related to the high levels of youth violence and aggression that are resulting from the many societal stressors on these children.

No matter what the cause, bullying creates stress in the schools. The reduction of bullying incidents appears to be related to two key factors: education of parents and effective school programs. Parents need to understand that bullying is not a normal part of growing up, because it can be extremely destructive to some young people. Educators often find strong resistance from parents whose children have been accused of bullying, either because these parents do not understand how serious the consequences can be for many children or because they feel their parenting skills are being attacked and become defensive. Parents have to pull their heads out of the sand and take steps within their own families to teach their children not to bully and to support their kids if they are being bullied. (Excellent resources for parents and educators are available at www.bullying.org.)

In light of this parental resistance, a more effective long-term approach to eliminating the "culture of bullying" would be better bullying prevention programs in the schools. Dr. Susan Limber, the associate director of the Institute on Family and Neighborhood Life at Clemson University, feels that the most effective anti-bullying strategies involve treating a school as a community in order to change the climate of the school and the norms of behavior that presently exist. In other words, all schools need to adopt programs

**The "Head-in-the-Sand" Approach**

Parents may inadvertently encourage bullying if they believe that:
- Bullying is a normal part of growing up.
- Children who bully will just grow out of it.
- Children are best left to resolve their own conflicts. They should learn to stick up for themselves. If my child fights back just once, the bullying will stop.
- My child thinks it will get worse if I tell, so begs for secrecy about bullying. I cannot tell the school.
- My child could never be a bully.

**Source: Pepler & Craig, *Making a Difference in Bullying* (2000).**

that do not just pay lip service to the problem, but that educate students over the long term about how to stop bullying. Such a program might be the Olweus Bullying Prevention Program developed by Norwegian psychologist Dan Olweus.

Along with these educational programs, school administrators need to take a strong stand in dealing with bullies in their schools. They cannot crumble under the weight of parental pressure when a bully has been identified. A zero-tolerance policy is required after a thorough investigation has determined that bullying has indeed been going on. Since the majority of bullying takes place in and around the school, this is where it needs to be stopped. But it can only be stopped if parents understand that they are the first line of defence: proper discipline at home can go a long way to eliminating bullying at school.

## What Constitutes Effective Discipline?

Parental confusion about the importance of discipline and, more importantly, how to discipline, must be cleared up so that children do not create chaos when they get into the classroom. The problem is that parents do not know where to begin. Many of the problems with family discipline in the past 50 years are that they focused so completely on eliminating the punitive aspects of discipline that they lost the positive aspects. The writings of experts, from Freud to Spock and even those of a modern writer like Penelope Leach, have caused parents not only to try to eliminate punishment, but to move past that point and become friends with their children. To the best of this author's knowledge, no parenting authority has actually advocated this. Positive discipline has become thoroughly confused with no discipline, with chaotic results. The entire subject of discipline needs to be clarified and simplified so that confusion is not getting in the way of direct action. Poor discipline is hurting both our children and our society, and it is time to remedy this problem.

## It Starts With the Relationship

The attachment that evolves between parents and their children forms the basis of the love that anchors their relationship. This deep attachment, which was discussed in Chapter 3, causes young children to want to do their parents' bidding. According to Dr. Leon Kuczynski of the University of Guelph, children's first desire is to please their parents. Initially they "obey with glee." The stronger this relationship, the more desire they have to please. It seems to follow, then, that it is important that parents spend as much time building this relationship as possible.

Initially the attachment or bond between children and their parents results from body contact. The newborn needs the warmth and comfort of body contact with the parents to feel safe and secure. As the child becomes mobile, first crawling, then walking, the relationship continues to grow through play. Parents love to make their children smile and laugh and to have fun with them. Through play the attachment continues to grow and increases the child's willingness and desire to please the parents.

It seems obvious that, the less time parents spend in play with their children, the weaker the bond between them and the weaker children's desire to do the parents' bidding. This might not make a huge difference at the infant level, but it could create major difficulties as the child gets older, especially if the parents lack the ability to set and to enforce clear limits.

Discipline with infants means little more than keeping them safe from harm. It means keeping them from putting their fingers and toys in electric sockets, from touching the hot oven door, and from handling breakable objects. Usually this takes the form of childproofing the house and removing infants from potentially dangerous situations.

As the children become mobile and are not always in direct contact with a parent, around the 18-month age, discipline begins to involve verbal instructions. It is at this point that the system can begin to break down. While children want to please their parents and will initially comply with these verbal instructions, such as "Don't hit your brother" or "Don't touch the plant," they soon begin to test the system. After being told not to touch the plant, they will often reach out towards it while at the same time watching the parent to see what the reaction will be. If told again, usually they will stop the offending behavior, but may possibly again test the parents' resolve. Usually a parent can settle the situation by simply repeating the command in a louder voice, or picking up the child and moving him or her to a safer location. Unfortunately, at this point many parents, believing perhaps that they are unfairly constraining their youngster's spirit, will give up and let the child continue with the undesired behavior.

The idea of early discipline is embodied in the concept of containment. This idea, as promoted by Dr. Tim Cavell of the University of Arkansas, suggests that young children want to be "contained," because it appears to help them to feel more secure. The combination of childproofing their environments and verbal instructions when they are misbehaving or doing something dangerous is a behavioral containment that not only provides a sense of security for the child, but also teaches them acceptable behavior.

Dr. Kuczynski, in a conversation with the author, noted that in positively functioning families, discipline is almost hidden, as it is seamlessly integrated into the parent-child relationship. In fact, "In normal families nothing disciplinary seems to be happening. [Parents] find that they are intervening for very small stuff. For example, at the table they might ask the child to 'Say Please.' It is not disciplinary; it's like a suggestion. You can have families almost without discipline when parents are there and seeing the small things. It [the interaction] can be occurring at a very harmonious level and preempting the need for discipline."

What makes this style of discipline work? It works because the parents are actually present to make the corrections in their children. Not a caregiver, not a daycare teacher, but the parents.

The flaw in this system, then, is immediately obvious. A parent needs to be available to "contain" the child. The child's love for the parents and basic willingness to comply combined with the parents' verbal instructions or physical removal from dangerous or antisocial situations are the key components of early discipline. If a parent is not present to do this, someone else has to. This other person will generally not be as strongly bonded to the child, and this decreases the child's willingness to comply. Furthermore, nonparental adults, such as daycare workers, are usually not as available to make the necessary behavioral corrections. The result will often be children who are more difficult to control when the parents return. If the parents can compensate by being very firm (although not angry) when the child is in their presence, then they will be able to maintain family discipline. If, on the other hand, they are confused as to their role, then the early forms of disobedience may be sowing the seeds of greater problems as the child gets older.

The key to early discipline, then, is in the relationship between parent and child. The bond between them is the reason the children want to do their parents' bidding. The correction of daily misdeeds and mistakes is the basis of the early forms of disciplining children, yet it does not really look like what most parents think of as discipline. Instead it is simply common sense containment. This approach relies heavily on parents being present to contain their children. If the parents rely on others to do this important job, then the results may be far different than they intend.

## Discipline is Teaching

As children get older and develop the ability to understand the reasons behind parental commands and instructions, parents must add explanations to the correction process. Remember, the purpose of discipline is to teach self-control. To do this teaching, then, parents must give reasons behind their actions or instructions. Without explanations, without children understanding why they should behave as requested, parents might control their children's behavior in the local setting, but will not necessarily extend their control to situations where they are away from the parents.

Keep these explanations short to avoid turning them into lectures, but do explain the reason behind the request or command. All one needs to say is, "Don't pull the cat's tail, it hurts the cat and makes him afraid of people. He won't be as friendly if you keep doing that." If the instruction plus a short explanation do not succeed in changing the behavior, a simple consequence needs to be added.

It is this addition of consequences to the disciplinary situation that has become so puzzling to parents. To avoid "punishing" their child, many parents believe that any type of consequence for misbehavior will harm their child. Nothing could be further from the truth. Most children will frequently test their parents' resolve by saying "no" to an instruction. If children do not comply after the parent repeats the instruction firmly, then a short time-out would be appropriate. There is no need for anger or yelling, but there is need for firm action to support the parent's direction. The consequence for children should be short, say, 15 minutes in their room for a tantrum or no dessert if they throw their food, along with the short explanation. Such a response should be enough to teach that the behavior is unacceptable. Repeated infractions may require slightly longer consequences, but parents need to keep in mind that children's memories are very short, and long penalties defeat the purpose as children will become restless and angry once they forget what the consequence was for.

## The Value of Consistency

Efforts to discipline children become extremely difficult if the corrections and consequences are not consistent. Children who are disciplined for a behavior one time and not the next cannot learn what is expected of them. Behavioral psychologists call this a "variable reinforcement schedule." A clear example occurs when a young child wants candy in a supermarket and throws a tantrum when denied that candy. If the parent gives in one time but refuses the next, how is the child to know when the tantrum will work and when it will not? A father might justify the behavior by saying that the first time the tantrum was disturbing a number of people, so he gave the candy to minimize the disruption, while the second time, no one was around so the candy was not given. Unfortunately this doesn't help the child to discriminate when the tantrum will work and when it won't. In the absence of clear guidelines and having obtained what was wanted on at least one occasion, the child will continue the behavior. It was variably rewarded.

On the other hand, when corrections or consequences are consistent, then learning occurs very quickly. Usually just two or three consistent responses are needed to teach the child that the particular behavior is unacceptable or that it will not achieve the desired end. Parents who wonder why their children are not responding to their disciplinary techniques should check their consistency for a common answer.

**A Modern Parent**

A young mother brought her 4-year-old daughter for a consultation. She explained that the daughter was a "stubborn" child who would not do what she was told. While the mother was explaining the problem, the youngster became restless, as most children of this age will, and started to interrupt her mother. To be able to continue the conversation, the mother took her daughter out into the waiting area to watch television. This she happily did, and a further 45 minutes was spent with the mom discussing the basics of discipline.

At the end of the session the mother went out to get her daughter, but she refused to leave. After several entreaties from her mother, the daughter crawled under a table and refused to come out. Would the mother apply the principles she had just spent an hour learning? She could not. The daughter would not come out. Finally the mother asked what to do. The answer was simple: Pick up her daughter and carry her out to the car. There was no need for anger, yelling, or bribery—just direct action. The mother did as suggested and the problem ended.

## Rules and Structure

Once children reach school age, the need for family rules becomes more important. While there should not be too many, a few simple rules that everyone understands help to keep the children safe and secure and to keep order in the household. Examples might be coming straight home after school, a clearly defined bedtime, and the type and amount of TV or video games allowed. Children cannot learn from rules that are made on the spot and are therefore constantly changing. "Instant" rules are often imposed in anger and the resulting rule may not be either fair or reasonable. Children who know what is expected of them feel more secure. They know where the boundaries are and are not surprised when consequences result from infractions.

Consequences for breaking these rules must be a part of the structure. While these consequences may not always be necessary if the child is sufficiently remorseful, older children usually require some reminder that they have broken the rules. These consequences must be administered immediately and they should again be of short duration. It does not take much to remind children that the family rules need to be followed, but some consequence for their misbehavior is usually necessary.

One important key to the setting of family rules is a yearly review. This is less necessary for young children in the 5 to 10 age group, but it is more important as the children get older. Each year parents should spend a few minutes with each child to review and possibly modify the rules. As children get older they can usually handle more freedom and later bedtimes. The first of September is usually a good time to do this review, as the return to school is to children what New Year's Day is to adults.

Parents need to understand that enforcing rules is much harder if children are coming home to an empty house. How can watching television, playing video games, or snacking on unhealthy foods be controlled if no one is there to supervise? While having both parents of school-age children working is generally a good thing for parents, some arrangement that allows one parent to be home when school ends is definitely preferable from a supervisory standpoint. Moreover, it helps communication and reinforces the bonds between parent and child.

## Setting an Example

As children get older their rules remain important, but a new factor is added: a respect for authority. Obeying their society's rules and laws—including their schools— becomes a vital component of functioning well in society. This respect for authority begins in the home, but must extend beyond it to include teachers and law enforcement officers. If parents do not set an example by showing respect for authority figures, then children will not either.

As discussed above, parental respect for teachers has been decreasing. Too often, parents of children who have been penalized for misbehavior march into the school ready for a fight and threaten to sue. The trouble these parents cause has been of such concern that school authorities, supported by the courts, have softened the penalties, for infractions, with the result that discipline in the schools is often in chaos. Such actions demonstrate to students that the decisions of teachers and school administrators are less than final—they are open for questioning and challenging.

The same argument also applies to peace officers and local security personnel. If a youngster is caught shoplifting, parents must support authorities rather than attack them for daring to arrest their child. Parents might believe that they are supporting their child and showing that they care. But what they are doing instead is lessening their child's respect for authority.

Respect for the law and the rules of society is one of civilization's essential features. Parents must model this respect if they expect their children to become good citizens. This parental modeling must also be evident by setting a good example when it comes to the parent's own respect for the law. Parents who consistently show little respect for authority figures, for the property of others, for traffic laws, or for their employer's property (such as office supplies) cannot expect their children to be law-abiding citizens merely because they tell them to be. A good example must be set for the kids to follow.

## The Role of Fathers

When we talk about the role of parents in teaching their children discipline, we must note that mothers and fathers play different roles in this process. Mothers are generally seen by their children as the nurturers and as the emotional hub of the family. It is to mother that children usually turn when their feelings are hurt or if they are physically hurt. It is not that fathers cannot fulfill this role, rather, it just seems that mothers are better at it. While this statement may offend many feminists, there is little doubt that the majority of the population understands that mothers are better nurturers than dads are.

A problem then arises if the mother also has to be the family disciplinarian. It is almost impossible to fill these two roles simultaneously. The nurturer has trouble switching hats from being the emotional supporter to becoming the disciplinarian as well. It is hard for the mother and confusing for the kids. This is where fathers become so important, especially with older children. Dads have traditionally been the family authority figure. "Wait 'til your father gets home" has been a well used warning throughout the centuries. There is good reason for this. Not only do fathers have a greater physical presence, with their deeper and louder voices and bigger muscles, but they also do not have to confuse the roles of nurturer and disciplinarian. It must be understood that in no way should discipline be physical. It is just that fathers, with their physical stature, usually tend to carry more authority when they are being firm.

This is not to say that fathers cannot be sympathetic and understanding with their children, but they are rarely as naturally good at this as mothers are. What then is wrong with the father taking an active part in the family by supporting the mother in disciplinary matters? It is a key family role and it is unfair for the mother to have to do everything, as they are now often doing. Discipline does not have to be done with anger or meanness; it just has to done effectively. In other words, the affection of the children for their father does not have to suffer just because he is the family's main authority figure. In fact, children who respect their parents have a much stronger relationship with them than those who don't.

When fathers spend time with their children and have fun with them, there is usually little need for other serious discipline measures other than these simple ones. However, when the children become teenagers and make inevitable impulsive or thoughtless mistakes, then it is vital that fathers take an active role in discussing the problem and meting out effective consequences. Fathers are generally more effective than mothers in this role, and it saves mothers from trying to be both the nurturer and disciplinarian. Mothers simply cannot do it all.

It is well and good to say that fathers should be integral to family discipline. But this piece of advice is challenged by a larger social trend that has seen the downgrading of the role of the father in the family. While there is some evidence that fathers have become more involved in caring for their very young children, by the time their children become teenagers, fathers in many families seem to fade from the picture.

Various studies have supported this conclusion. For example, fewer than 20 percent of Ontario students in Grades 7 to 12 said they could talk to their fathers about their problems, as opposed 40 percent who could speak to their mothers. A *Reader's Digest* poll of Canadian teenagers found that mothers are much more involved in their teenagers' lives than are fathers. Many fathers did not even know the names of their teenagers' friends.

My own clinical work has also pointed to the phenomenon of the "vanishing father." Many of the teenagers that I see for counseling prove to have uninvolved fathers, both in intact families and divorced ones. Such a lack of involvement has two effects. First, it increases the stress on mothers. Stressed mothers, most of whom are at work all day, have less patience with their teens and tend to have more confrontations with them. Second, it increases the anger felt by teens. Those adolescents whose fathers are not taking an active part in their lives tend to be angrier and show more behavior problems—both at home and at school—than do those with involved fathers. These teens communicate their frustrations by skipping school, using drugs (and often leaving the paraphernalia around to be found), and flouting the family rules. Usually they do not themselves know why they are angry until they get to a counseling situation.

Many studies confirm the importance of the father's role in the family not only for disciplinary purposes, but also for a wide range of other factors. Research by the National Center for Education Statistics in the United States shows that the fathers' attentiveness to teenage children was strongly related to their school performance. Other studies indicate that children adjust better to divorce when their fathers stay involved in their lives. There is even evidence that shows that girls with uninvolved or absent fathers are more likely to become pregnant as teens.

There is no question that fathers are a vital part of their children's lives, so why are fathers becoming less involved in their families? A major reason is that fathers are working longer and harder at their jobs. For the most part, they are still the main earners in most families and tend to be the ones who put in the most job hours. When children are young the fathers are usually younger, too, and are just starting their careers. That's when they often have time to be an active parent. Thirteen or so years later, when the children are in their teens, the fathers are usually well established in their careers, often having taken on more responsibility and more hours. The result is that they are not around the home as much, and when they are, they lack the energy that discipline requires. It takes time and energy to communicate with and discipline children, and many fathers have neither of these. That leaves the moms to bear the burden of running the family. These moms are often out in the working world, facing the same kinds of pressures as the fathers. In these cases, the teens are even less well-off since they now lack both a dad and a mom as a strong presence in their lives.)

The importance of discipline in the family and the key role that the lack of it is playing in many of the problems our youth, were articulated by clinical psychologist Dr. Maggie Mamen in her book, *The Pampered Child Syndrome: How to Recognize It, How to Manage It, and How to Avoid It*. Mamen's book targeted the advice parents have been receiving from "well-meaning professionals" and children's rights activists to use child-centered parenting strategies. By this she means "allowing children to make their own choices and set their own limits." But this advice has backfired, she argues. Rather than raising independent children, society is raising "a generation of pampered children who have an exaggerated sense of entitlement, who have no respect for authority, and who are being diagnosed with and treated for a broadening range of psychiatric disorders—often by the very same professionals who are promoting the child-driven approaches to parenting."

With their parents pampering them rather than disciplining them, "these children expect to be kept happy and stimulated, to be treated equally to adults, and to be in charge. When they run into situations that challenge these expectations, they have difficulty coping, and may show symptoms of depression, anxiety, hyperactivity or behaviour disorders. Their parents are often at a loss to understand why their children are so unhappy, when they have always been given everything they wanted."

This is the situation in a nutshell. Parents must take a new look at discipline, in a simplified and clarified form, if they are to expect their children to be secure and confident members of society.

# CHAPTER VII

# Media and Technology

I t seems ironic that the fruits of modern science that were designed to entertain and inform are also creating so much stress in the younger generation. While television, computers, the Internet, and video games are certainly fulfilling their entertainment purpose, they are also creating problems for our youth in many different areas. The scope of the potential problems can be seen in a report by the United States Federal Trade Commission that showed that a typical American child in 2001 spent an average of over 38 hours a week using these entertainment media. This was much longer than they spend in school in the same time period, and was in fact longer than children spent doing anything else except sleeping.

That children sit mesmerized in front of a screen for over five hours a day on average is bad enough. Compounding the problem is the almost complete absence of any parental control over their children's media exposure. Given that young people lack maturity both to realize the damage they are doing to themselves, and to control themselves, parents must begin to take a more active role in monitoring their children's use of modern technologies and understand its impacts.

## Television

Of the whopping total of 38 hours that kids spend using various electronic media—television, web magazines, CDs, MP3s, and so forth—about 25 hours are spent watching TV. Of equal concern to the number of hours kids are spending viewing TV is the lack of parental monitoring of what their children are actually watching. In one American survey of children between 8 and 18, fewer than two of five families had any rules about what the kids could watch. A survey conducted for the Canadian Teacher's Federation showed that by the time they reach Grade 6, half of the children reported that they had watched "unsuitable" movies on video and that their parents did not limit how much TV they watched or what they can watch. One reason for this lack of parental monitoring is the large number of children with televisions in their own rooms. One study estimated that 20 percent of children age 2 to 7 had their own televisions, with the proportion rising to 46 percent for 8 to 12 year olds, and 56 percent for 13 to 17 year olds. In Canada the CTF survey showed that almost half of all children age 8 to 15 controlled their own televisions.

Having multiple television sets in a household results in the privatization of viewing. In other words, adults watch one TV while children watch on a separate one. In fact, one survey found that 85 percent of the time that children watch television, there are no parents in the room. If parents are unaware of what their children are watching, then they will be equally unaware of what effects this extensive viewing has on their children. According to a huge volume of recent research, these effects can be substantial, particularly in terms of violence and sex.

## Violence

For many years the debate has raged about whether the media really do have any negative influence on children. Perhaps the biggest debate has been over what influence watching violent events on television or in the movies has on young children. Parents no longer need to have any doubts. Research has now shown that violence in the media has a clear and measurable effect on young children.

The clearest indication of this came in July 2000, when six major organizations dealing with children issued a "Joint Statement on the Impact of Entertainment Violence on Children" to a Congressional Public Health Summit in Washington, D.C. The American Academy of Pediatrics, American Medical Association, American Academy of Child and Adolescent Psychiatry, American Psychological Association, American Academy of Family Physicians, and the American Psychiatric Association reviewed over 1000 studies that showed an overwhelming causal connection between media violence and aggressive behavior in some children. This major segment of the public health community concluded that viewing entertainment violence can lead to increases in aggressive attitudes, values, and behavior in children. The measurable negative effects reported in this joint statement were found to take the following forms:

- Children who see a lot of violence are more likely to view violence as an effective way of settling conflicts

- Children regularly exposed to violence are more likely to assume that acts of violence are acceptable behavior

- Viewing violence can lead to emotional desensitization towards violence in real life

- Viewing violence can decrease the likelihood that one will take action on behalf of a victim when violence occurs

- Entertainment violence feeds a perception that the world is a violent and mean place

- Viewing violence increases one's fear of becoming a victim of violence, with a resultant increase in self-protective behaviors and a mistrust of others

- Viewing violence may lead to real-life violence, as children exposed to violent programming at a young age have a higher tendency for violent and aggressive behavior later in life than do children who are not so exposed

To understand the magnitude of this problem, one study in 1992 estimated that by the time a teenager was 18, she will have witnessed on television 200,000 acts of violence including 40,000 murders. The really sad part of this figure is that according to the National Television Violence Study, 46 percent of all television violence took place in children's cartoons.

While many children will be able to tell the difference between cartoon violence and real life, there is research evidence to show that dangers do exist. The way in which the violence is portrayed in cartoons may suggest to children that violence is the best or only way to resolve interpersonal conflicts. For example, in an early study, children who were shown Batman and Superman cartoons over a four-week period were more likely to fight, break toys, and play roughly than a control group that had watched Mr. Rogers' Neighborhood. Moreover, children in the control group were more cooperative and willing to share with others. Even more telling is that this research showed that three-quarters of all the television violence went unpunished. This gives the message that violence has no consequences, which is a very dangerous conclusion for children to draw.

All of this research raises the very obvious question: *If this worrisome information is out there, why are they not taking more steps to limit their children's exposure to violence in the media?* The answer appears to be that parents are actually unaware of these important statistics. A study by Anderson and Bushman showed that news reports about the effects of media violence were watered down so as to imply that there is not that much evidence against the viewing of violence at all. Apparently the media do not want it known that the violence they are showing is bad for children. To find this information, parents would need to take the time and effort to search it out in the research. Unfortunately, as we have made it clear throughout this book, parents are too busy working and taking care of their own needs to take the time to research something that would contribute to their parenting abilities or their children's welfare.

Even worse, even if parents wanted to obtain accurate information, they would find that many in the media are actively marketing their violent material to parents and children alike. In the words of the U.S. Federal Trade Commission:

> the practice of pervasive and aggressive marketing of violent motion pictures, recorded music and electronic games to children undermines the credibility of the industries ratings and labels and frustrates parents' attempts to make informed decisions about their children's exposure to violent content.

Put differently, despite a labeling system that would indicate otherwise, the media themselves are marketing their products so as to make them seem less violent than they are and thus highly attractive to youngsters.

The evidence is clear, violence in the media effects children. Certainly not all children become violent from watching television or movies, but those effected are likely to be children from difficult family situations or whose parents spend little time with them. A 1986 study showed that aggression in first graders can be reduced through an educational program that helps them to change their attitude toward media violence. This indicates that educational programs in the schools or parental instruction in the home could be instrumental in countering the effects of violence in the media. But for this to happen, the parents must become involved.

## Sex

In 2004, a survey by the Kaiser Family Foundation showed that parents are even more concerned about the amount of sex being shown in the media than they are about violence. Parents certainly have cause for this concern as there is little doubt that there is more sex in movies and on television than ever before. Confirmation of this statement comes from the Kid Risk Project at the Harvard School of Public Health, which found that over the past ten years movies have become more violent, more sexual and more profane. In terms of sex, this research found significant increases in sexual content in movies rated PG, PG-13, and R. The study concluded that the Motion Picture Association of America, the group that rates movies in the United States, has become "increasingly more lenient in assigning its age-based movie ratings."

Does seeing more sex in today's media shape the sexual behavior in children? Apparently yes, according to a study reported in the prestigious journal *Pediatrics*. In a longitudinal study of almost 1800 adolescents between 12 and 17 years of age, the study concluded that teenagers who view sexual content on television, even if it only involves characters talking about sex, are twice as likely to begin having intercourse in the following year as are peers who do not view such content. It also showed that sexual content on TV was more likely to speed up adolescents' movement from milder sexual behavior, such as breast fondling or genital touching, to more serious sexual actions such as oral sex or intercourse. One of the problems noted by the authors of this research was that the sexual content of these programs and movies rarely shows any negative outcomes of having sex. In other words, the media rarely show girls getting pregnant, participants getting sexually transmitted diseases, or anyone suffering from feelings of guilt after a one-night stand. No wonder adolescents (and even younger children) are having more sex after viewing explicit TV shows and movies if everyone seems to be doing it and nothing bad ever happens.

The real tragedy is that a very large percentage of parents surveyed recognized that television shows contained too much bad language and sexual content. In a national survey by Public Agenda in 2002, about 90 percent of adults said that television programs were getting worse every year because of bad language and adult themes in shows that air from 8 to 10 p.m. In Britain, 86 percent of respondents to a BBC poll feel that their government should step in to regulate sexually explicit television and magazine images aimed at children.

If so many people think this way, why do they not vote with their remote controls? If no one were to watch these programs, the producers would very quickly change the content to what people want. The advertisers would insist on it. Parents cannot just wait for the government to act; they have to take action themselves. They can do this by not watching the programs, by not allowing their kids to watch the shows, and by letting their government representatives know how they feel. This, of course, is easier said than done.

> For the 2001–02 TV season, 64 percent of all programs had sexual content; 61 percent included sex-related talk; with overt portrayals of sex at 32 percent. Those shows with sexual content included 4.4 sex scenes per hour. And over all, 1 out of every 7 programs included a portrayal of sexual intercourse.
>
> **Source: Pediatrics 114, no. 3 (September 2004)**

The reality is that most parents do not know what their kids are watching and even if they did, it takes too much energy for many to actually set limits on their children's TV and movie habits. Many parents either do not want to upset their kids by setting these limits or they do not have the energy for the battles they know they are going to have. Neither of these are very good excuses considering the powerful effect that these media sources are having on their children.

Moreover, according to Dr. Rebecca Collins, the lead author of the *Pediatrics* study on sexuality cited above, parents have a real opportunity to shape not only the images their children see on television but also their sexual behavior. Collins argued that parents who control the amount of sexual content their children are exposed to can make a significant difference in how quickly they develop sexually. According to the statistics reported, 46 percent of all high school students in the United States have had sexual intercourse, and 1 of every 4 sexually active students gets a sexually transmitted disease. This may not seem too alarming to parents until it is realized that these figures include students from Grade 9 to 12. By the time they are in Grade 12, over 80 percent of the students have had intercourse. These are very high figures and are definitely too high for the number of adolescents who are actually ready for sex. A combination of limiting the sexual content of the media with parental limits on what can be watched would more than likely have a significant effect on lowering these figures.

## The V-chip and Ratings Systems

There is some good news for parents who really are interested in limiting the content of the television and movies that their children are watching. All the necessary technology now exists to easily limit this content, even when the parents are not at home. The V-chip is a technology that lets parents block television programming they do not want their children to watch. Most television shows, in both Canada and the U.S. now include a rating of their content. (The rating appears in the corner of your television screen during the first 15 seconds of a program and in TV programming guides.) The rating system, also known as "TV Parental Guidelines," was established by the National Association of Broadcasters, the National Cable Television Association, and the Motion Picture Association of America. (A Canadian rating system has also been developed.) This rating is encoded into the programs, and the V-chip technology reads the encoded information and blocks shows accordingly. Using the remote control, parents can program the V-chip to block certain shows based on their ratings.

As of January 1, 2000, the U.S. Federal Communications Commission (FCC) required all new television sets 13 inches or larger to contain the V-chip technology. If you want a V-chip but do not want to buy a new television, you can get a set-top box, which works the same as a built-in V-chip. Personal computers that include a television tuner and a monitor of 13 inches or greater are also required to include V-chip technology.

The U.S. rating system is as follows:

- *TV-Y (All Children) — This program is designed to be appropriate for all children. Whether animated or live-action, the themes and elements in this program are specifically designed for a very young audience, including children from ages 2-6. This program is not expected to frighten younger children.*

- *TV-Y7 (Directed to Older Children) — This program is designed for children age 7 and above. It may be more appropriate for children who have acquired the developmental skills needed to distinguish between make-believe and reality. Themes and elements in this program may include mild fantasy or comedic violence, or may frighten children under the age of 7. Therefore, parents may wish to consider the suitability of this program for their very young children. Note: For those programs where fantasy violence may be more intense or more combative than other programs in this category, such programs will be designated TV-Y7-FV.*

- *TV-G (General Audience) — Most parents would find this program suitable for all ages. Although this rating does not signify a program designed specifically for children, most parents may let younger children watch this program unattended. It contains little or no violence, no strong language, and little or no sexual dialogue or situations.*

- *TV-PG (Parental Guidance Suggested) — This program contains material that parents may find unsuitable for younger children. Many parents may want to watch it with their younger children. The theme itself may call for parental guid-*

*ance and the program might contain one or more of the following: moderate violence (V), some sexual situations (S), infrequent coarse language (L), or some suggestive dialogue (D).*

*• TV-14 (Parents Strongly Cautioned) — This program contains some material that many parents would find unsuitable for children under 14 years of age. Parents are strongly urged to exercise greater care in monitoring this program and are cautioned against letting children under the age of 14 watch unattended. This program contains one or more of the following: intense violence (V), intense sexual situations (S), strong coarse language (L), or intensely suggestive dialogue (D).*

*• TV-MA (Mature Audience Only) — This program is specifically designed to be viewed by adults and therefore may be unsuitable for children under 17. This program contains one or more of the following: graphic violence (V), explicit sexual activity (S), or crude indecent language (L).*

As mentioned above these ratings are automatically broadcast with each program. Parents just need to set what type of programming they want to block with their remote control units and that programming will not appear. While the majority of television shows watched in Canada are of American origin, and therefore follow the U.S. rating system, there are also some programs of Canadian origin. To cover this situation a Canadian rating system has been developed, and most new television sets sold in Canada have their V-chips programmed for this system (in both French and English) as well. Inclusion of the Canadian English and French program classification systems in television sets is not a regulatory or legislative requirement, but most television set manufacturers have begun to add these Canadian rating systems to their V-chip technology on a voluntary basis. The Canadian code is somewhat less complicated, but also includes less detail. It is:

*E – Exempt*

*C – Children*

*C 8+ – Children 8 years of age and older*

*G – General Programming, suitable for all audiences*

*PG – Parental Guidance*

*14+ – Viewers 14 years and older*

*18+ – Adult Programming*

Helpful though they are, the combination of the V-chip and the two ratings systems do not solve all parental concerns. One problem appears to be the complexity of the American ratings system. Many parents do not understand what the various ratings guidelines mean. According to one survey, only 28 percent of parents of young children (2-6 years old) knew what the rating TV-Y7 meant (directed to children age 7 and older) while 13 percent thought it meant the exact opposite (directed to children under 7). Only 12 percent knew that the rating FV (fantasy violence) was related to violent content; 8 percent thought it means "family viewing." By contrast, the Canadian system suffers from its simplicity. For example, if G-rated programs are suitable for all ages, why bother having a "C" or a "C8+" rating at all?

Another problem is that most parents just don't bother to take the time to set the V-chip to block programs they do not want their children to watch. Part of this problem might be technophobia. If setting the time on a VCR was difficult for many people, programming a V-chip would be impossible, especially on the multiple brands of sets that are in most households.

A third problem is that many parents fear a backlash from their children. "All my friends can watch those shows," children will complain, and parents lack energy or even conviction to maintain their standards.

Finally, and perhaps most disturbing, many parents simply do not realize the potential damage these violent and sex-filled shows can cause. As a result, they do not bother to set their V-chips either.

In short, the technology exists to limit the violent and sexual content that children and adolescents can watch in their homes. It is up to the parents to actually use this technology to protect their kids.

## Reading, Academic Achievement and the Importance of Play

The increasingly long hours that young children are spending watching television not only influences their behavior but also influences their reading ability and their potential academic achievement. There is no doubt that there can be positive effects of limited viewing of such well-designed educational programs as Sesame Street on young children, especially those from impoverished backgrounds. Studies have shown, however, that children who watch cartoons or other strictly entertainment-oriented television shows during their pre-school years have poorer pre-reading skills at age 5. There appear to be two reasons for these results.

First, while children are watching entertaining television programs, they are not playing, either by themselves or with other children. This is a significant problem because play, particularly make-believe play, has been shown to contribute to the development of a wide variety of higher mental functions that are important for later academic achievement. These functions include:

- General Cognitive and Social Skills—Preschoolers who spend more time in dramatic play with other children are advanced in general intellectual development and are viewed as being more socially competent by their teachers. Young children who especially enjoy pretending also score higher on tests of imagination and creativity.

- Memory—Studies show that fantasy play strengthens children's memory. Play may provide a vital foundation for more sophisticated memory strategies later in child-hood.

• Language and Literacy—Language facility has been shown to be enriched by play experiences. Play appears to be a way in which all facets of conversational dialogue can be improved. It also helps children's early literacy development as time children spend pretending at age 4 has been shown to be positively related to the development of reading and writing skills in later schooling.

• Reasoning—Make-believe helps to foster young children's ability to reason about impossible or absurd situations.

While parents undoubtedly realize that these cognitive skills are vital for future academic achievement, few understand that they can be significantly improved through play. Watching television entertains children rather than allows them to entertain themselves through fantasy and pretending, and thus limits cognitive development.

A second problem associated with television viewing by young children is the decrease in attention span. A study in the April 2004 edition of *Pediatrics* showed television might overstimulate the brain and permanently "rewire" it as it is developing. For every hour of television watched in a day, the children (one group of 1-year olds, a second group of 3-year olds) were found to have a 10 percent increased risk of having attention problems at age 7. In other words, children who watched 3 to 4 hours of television a day had a 30 to 40 percent increased risk of attention problems. These findings help to explain why there has been such a huge increase in children with attention deficit disorder in the last decade.

For older children who are already in school, television takes away potential reading hours. Reading is the key to success in all academic subject areas, and children are no longer spending the hours in books that they once did. School librarians are finding that

The April, 2004 *Pediatrics* study involved 1345 children and not only showed the increased potential for attention problems but also shed light on how much TV young children were watching. The figures for each group were:

**One-Year-Olds**

No TV: 36%

1 – 2 hrs/day: 37%

3 – 4 hrs/day: 14%

5+ hrs/day: 13%

**Three-Year-Olds**

No TV: 7%

1 – 2 hrs/day: 44%

3 –4 hrs/day: 27%

5 – 6 hrs/day: 11%

7+ hrs/day: 10%

These are very high figures, especially for the three-year-olds. Is there any doubt that TV watching has become a major problem for children?

fewer and fewer students are signing out books and many libraries are turning from being book-lending facilities to being media centers, where students come to do research on computers. Reading increases vocabulary, factual knowledge, and stimulates the imagination. If children are watching television instead of reading, they limit their potential.

## War & Tragedy

Finally, the advent of satellite communications and all-news television channels means that every major disaster in every corner of the world can be seen on a daily basis in "real time." This has not always been the case. News about the Second World War could only be seen on a weekly basis on movie newsreels. Even then, this news was heavily censored to reflect only the most positive side of the war to minimize its impact on the home population. This trend began to change in the late 1960s with reporting on the war in Vietnam. More war correspondents with television cameras were present on the battlefields to tape the devastation and carnage, and this was not being censored. The result was that television coverage had a major impact on popular feelings about the war, especially with young people, and played a major part in its eventual end. Even then, the tapes had to be flown back to the U.S., which limited the number that could be shown.

Today every earthquake, explosion, flood, or local war can be shown immediately on the daily news broadcasts. Young people watching the daily litany of disaster and death are often strongly

## What Should Parents Be Doing About Their Children's Media Watching?

To gain some control over their children's media experiences, parents should:

- ✓ Know the shows your children see.
- ✓ Limit television use to 1 or 2 *quality* hours per day.
- ✓ Set situation limits (such as no TV or video games before school or before homework is done).
- ✓ Keep television and video game machines out of children's bedrooms.
- ✓ Turn the TV off during mealtimes.
- ✓ Turn the TV on only when there is something specific you have decided is worth watching, not to "see if there's something on."
- ✓ Use the V-chip technology to limit the violent and sexual content that their children watch.
- ✓ Watch what your children are watching.
- ✓ Be an active viewer, talking and making connections with your children while the program is on.
- ✓ Learn about movies that are playing and the videos available for rental or purchase.
- ✓ Be explicit with your children about your guidelines for appropriate movie viewing and review proposed movie choices in advance.
- ✓ Set a good example and limit your own TV viewing.

On the flip side, parents should not:

- ✗ Use television, videos, or video games as a babysitter.
- ✗ Place the TV in the most prominent location in your home.

American Medical Association, *Physician Guide to Media Violence* (1996).

influenced by these media images as the sheer volume of negativity gives the sense that the world is a chaotic and dangerous place. While this is true in some parts of the world, it is not usually the case in Canada or the United States, yet it causes many young people, especially the more sensitive ones, to worry about such problems as world peace, pollution, and climate change. Of course children should understand some aspects of these problems, but their relative youth and immaturity cause them stress and concern when they are unable to do anything about these situations.

This is not an easy problem for parents to deal with. There is no returning to a world of blissful ignorance or government censorship. Instead instant communications are here to stay. Parents should be alert, however, to the fact that their children may be stressed by the world's problems and be available to discuss these natural and man-made disasters with them. If their children routinely watch the news, then parents should watch with them so as to be available to answer questions and to reassure their children that most of these problems cannot happen here. Children can be much more disturbed by world events than parents realize and parents should not simply dismiss the possibility that their children could be affected by these remote happenings.

## Technology

Today's children are not only sitting in front of television screens but also computer screens. Children's exposure to and familiarity with computer technology can be rather surprising, with kindergartners able to "surf the Net" with utter ease. By the time children are in middle school, they can be fully immersed in the world of video games, online chat rooms, and music downloading programs. Such involvement often occurs without the complete (or sometimes, any) understanding by parents. Not surprisingly, this technological knowledge gap between child and parent can create much stress in the home. Let's examine, then, some of the issues involved in these technologies, with an eye toward helping parents gain a handle on the merits and dangers of their children's computer experiences.

## The Internet

Few technological innovations have changed so many aspects of life as has the explosive development of the Internet. What was once a defense-oriented chain of American university computers that could only be accessed via a thorough knowledge of complex computer languages is now a world-wide network among millions of computers accessible by almost anyone. The two areas of life most effected by this linkage are communications and knowledge retrieval. The ability to send instant messages and letters around the world has made it mandatory for all businesses and even most homes to be connected to this network. "Snail mail" has become almost obsolete in most modern countries and soon even the telephone system will be via the Internet. Wireless technology has made it possible to communicate instantly from anywhere that has cellular telephone service, from a device as small as a package of cigarettes.

Knowledge retrieval has revolutionized the scholarly world by making vast amounts of information accessible from home. Where once a university library was the only place to find the necessary information for serious essays, theses, and dissertations, every home now has access to the necessary data. Students no longer need to use their school or local libraries to find the books containing the information they require and so do not have to face the problems involved with lost books or those already taken out by other students. (Of course, even if they wanted to use the school libraries, those libraries have been turned into technology centers rather than book centers.) Unfortunately, these wonderful changes in life, derived from rapid improvements in communication technology, have also created some new problems for young people and their parents.

## Chat Lines

One of the most common concerns expressed by parents about the Internet is the tendency of most young people today to use chat lines instead of the telephone. Teens, especially girls, prefer to use such facilities as MSN to talk to each other because it allows so many different people to be involved in the conversation at once. Chat lines also allow the teens freer expression as they can say things on-line that they could never say to a person face-to-face. Still, Internet chat does not come without its share of problems. These include:

- **Chat line addiction**. Children can actually become addicted to the chat lines. Some children, mostly teenagers, are spending more than 3 hours a day "talking" on the computer. In past generations teens had a similar problem with overusing the telephone, but never to the addiction level. This addiction means that the teens are not interacting with their families, not getting any exercise, and often not getting their homework done. Interestingly, adults can have this same addiction. There is something about this method of communication that is addictive and parents need to be alert for signs of this problem.

- **Cyberbullying**. The phenomenon of cyberbullying occurs when a group of kids gangs up on another over the chat lines. It has long been known that children can be cruel to each other, but the relative anonymity of not having to face the person or talk directly to him or her has made it easier for children to verbally abuse others. For this reason the taunts can be far more devastating than they would be face-to-face. This isolates the bullied child as he or she (it is more often females who are bullied this way) can no longer use the chat lines for fear of the consequences.

• **Sexual predation**. Chat lines have become a favorite way for sexual predators to meet their victims. Once again the anonymity of this method of communication allows adult pedophiles to act as teens to gain a child's trust. Once this has occurred a meeting will eventually be arranged where rape, kidnapping and even murders have resulted. Parents should not minimize this danger. It has become such a big a problem that police have set up special units to trap these predators.

## Pornography

One of the most dangerous aspects of the Internet, especially for boys, is the ready availability of all types of pornography. Once available only in magazines, which were hard to buy for teens and even harder to hide, now virtually everything in the sexual world is available in graphic detail with just a few keystrokes. A certain amount of sexual curiosity in young males is certainly to be expected, but for some youngsters the curiosity can become an addiction that can have several potentially harmful effects.

The first of these effects is the way that pornography portrays women. It desensitizes young men to women's feelings and reduces women to the level of sexual objects. Also, many of these addicted young people have reported that the pornography, usually accompanied by masturbation, becomes sex for them and causes them to lose interest in real girls entirely.

Another effect of heavy pornography viewing is that it can create a perception of sex that focuses far too much on the physical rather than the emotional and romantic. Feelings and emotions are not part of pornography, and that could cause heavy users to think that there is nothing more to a relationship than casual, erotic sex. It also creates a perception of normal sexuality that is not normal at all but mostly fantasy. The acts, clothing, sex toys, and positions depicted do not normally exist in the average bedroom with the possible result that real sex could be perceived as comparatively boring.

As with chat line addiction, a pornography fixation also causes social isolation, both from the family and friends and can also result in feelings of inferiority and depression. While this is not the most common of the Internet problems, it is certainly the one that raises the most concern among parents, and is potentially one of the most emotionally crippling for young boys.

## Gambling

Gambling has been gaining in popularity among teenagers for a number of years, just as it has with adults. The proliferation of state and provincial lotteries, sports pools, bingo halls, and casinos has made gambling a legitimate pastime. These common gambling forms, however, are difficult for teens as most jurisdictions have made it illegal for them to participate. They cannot legally buy lottery or sports pool tickets or enter a bingo hall or casino. While they certainly find their way around these obstacles often enough, nothing is easier than gambling on the Internet. A recent count found over 1400 gambling sites available for use. These sites make excellent use of video graphics and appear much the same as video games to young people.

The only obstacle to gambling on the Internet is the need for a credit card number to put up the necessary stakes. Unfortunately this is no problem for many older teens who have a job, since credit

> "Statistics prove that teenage Internet gambling is the fastest growing addiction of the day, akin to drug and alcohol abuse in the 1930s."
>
> **David Robertson, former chairman of the National Coalition Against Legalized Gambling. March 17, 2002, CNN.com/Health**

card companies are all too pleased to issue them with one. Other teenagers must resort to stealing their parents' card numbers, which in turn has to be covered up by stealing the monthly statements. While in these cases it does not take long for parents to discover the problem, it also does not take long for the teen to acquire a huge debt.

Though this problem is still small, it is growing and parents must become more vigilant about how their children are using the Internet. (Parents also must become more vigilant about their credit card statements, checking that they know about all the purchases recorded each month.)

## Video Games

The last issue for parents regarding computer technology is the transformation of computer and video games from a harmless diversion to a dangerous influence. Video games have actually been present in society for over 30 years now. The original game was the simple but entertaining Pong, which appeared in 1972 and simulated a ping-pong game on a video screen. These games were originally only available in arcades, because home computers had not yet been invented. As these computers began slowly to enter homes in the 1980s, games such as Pacman and Space Invaders became popular with children and parents alike. These games also aroused no initial concern because the graphic ability of the early computers only allowed relatively crude figures, such as a yellow ball with a mouth or saucer-like object that represented a space ship. While shooting did occur in some of these games no human figures were involved so the games were rightly considered to be harmless entertainment.

The harmless aspects of these games changed rapidly in the 1990s as technology, and the improvement in computer graphics specifically, made rapid strides to the point where extremely realistic scenarios could be depicted. Even more important, these games were no longer confined to expensive home computers but were designed to be played on small, dedicated game machines that almost everyone could afford. The combination of realism and affordability proved to be so effective that worldwide video game sales alone are estimated to be over $20 billion per year. Video games are now so popular that a 2002 study found that the average American child plays these games for 7 hours a week. This figure is bad enough but when broken down by sex, they discovered that adolescent girls play about 5 hours a week while boys play an average of 13 hours in the same time frame. If these are the averages, the mind boggles at what the upper end of the scale must be.

As these changes both in graphic content and in popularity have burst upon the children's entertainment scene, parents and researchers have recently become concerned about the effects on their children. In particular, they are concerned about the levels of violence. An analysis of the content of video games done by Children Now in 2001 showed that almost 90 percent contained some violent content, and about half the games include serious violent content towards other game characters. Many of the new games, such as Grand Theft Auto (San Andreas), Counter-Strike, and Manhunt are incredibly violent.

As these games have developed, researchers have recognized a parallel between the effects on children that violence on television has been shown to have and the possibility of similar effects from video games. An analysis of 35 different studies by Anderson and Bushman found a clear and consistent pattern among the research: exposure to violent video games damages children academically, physiologically, socially, emotionally, and cognitively.

## Academic Damage.

A 2004 investigation found that a large number of studies have shown a negative association between the amount of video game play and school performance for children, adolescents, and even college students. In other words, the more video games played, the lower the grades. After all, those 7 hours a week that the average child is playing video games are 7 hours that the child is not reading, doing homework, or engaging in other creative activities. And not surprisingly, those spending more than the average are in the most danger as time for intellectual activities disappears as the hours playing video games increases.

## Physiological Damage.

Several studies found that exposure to violent video games increases physiological arousal. Playing these games increased heart rate and blood pressure by releasing the hormones involved in the stress response. This explains why children are much more irritable after long periods of playing violent games.

## Social Damage.

Exposure to violent video games decreases prosocial (helping) actions. In other words, children who play these games do not get along as well with other children. After all, most violent video games require the player to hurt, kill, destroy, and otherwise overwhelm the "enemy." Games reward such violent strategies, by awarding points for killing the bad guys or moving the player to a higher level after blowing up the enemy. Furthermore, violence is presented as justified and enjoyable and worse, without any negative consequences. There are rarely opportunities for cooperative solutions; the player either wins or loses, but can never compromise. Obviously, children playing such games cannot help but learn that the only solution to a problem is to fight it out until he wins—not the kind of lesson parents should want their children to learn.

## Emotional Damage.

The damage to a child's emotional well-being is perhaps the most disturbing aspect of violent video games. The problems in this area include:

- **Increased aggressive thoughts**. These findings were not only for males, but for females as well. Even adults showed the same results.

- **Increased aggressive emotions**. Findings show that children are more moody and aggressive i.e. in a bad mood, after playing these games.

• **Increased aggressive actions**. Not only do children develop aggressive thoughts, they often translate these thoughts into actions such as frequent arguments with teachers or being involved in physical fights.

• **Emotional Desensitization.** Events that should normally bring a strong emotional response instead prompt a numbed or blunted response. An example might be a suicide bombing that kills a large number of people. While most people would react with horror, serious gamers would react very little to such an event, if at all.

## Cognitive Damage.

Playing video games can desensitize one's cognitive abilities to the point where, rather than thinking that violence is uncommon and unlikely, children think that it is actually mundane and inevitable. In other words gamers begin to take the attitude that violence is everywhere and that nothing can be done about it. When this desensitization occurs it seems to change the moral code of serious video gamers so that their ideas of right and wrong become confused.

Given this range of evidence, parents might ask whether video games are actually worse than television. The response, according to many researchers is, in fact, yes. Psychologists Barbara Krahe and Ingrid Moller of the University of Potsdam in Germany summarized how video games have more serious effects than television or movies:

• They provide direct rewards, such as points or promotion to the next game level, to the players for their aggressive actions in the game.

• They facilitate the rehearsal of specific behavioral skills, such as killing a character with a gun.

• They help the gamer to identify with the aggressor by allowing players to choose from a range of characters.

- They are characterized by increasing realism in graphics and sound, combined with even more extreme violent action.

Remember, violent video games appear to be even worse for children than violent television or movies. This is likely because of the interactive nature of these games. The players themselves become the main characters of the games and so become the ones being violent. This is not the case in TV or the movies where the actors are the ones being violent. (Of course, parents should not read this and conclude that television is not so bad. As we discussed above, it *is* bad. It is just that video games are even worse.)

To deflect some of the criticism now being leveled at violent video games, the video game industry has established the Entertainment Software Rating Board (ESRB). This is a self-regulatory body for the interactive entertainment software industry established in 1994 by the Entertainment Software Association. This board has established a rating system so that parents can instantly recognize the type of content in a game and presumably exercise some control over which ones their children purchase. The system includes the following categories:

**EARLY CHILDHOOD.** Titles rated **EC—Early Childhood** have content that may be suitable for ages 3 and older. Contains no material that parents would find inappropriate.

**EVERYONE.** Titles rated **E—Everyone** have content that may be suitable for persons ages 6 and older. Titles in this category may contain minimal violence, some comic mischief, and mild language.

**TEEN.** Titles rated **T—Teen** have content that may be suitable for persons ages 13 and older. These games may contain violent content, mild or strong language, and suggestive themes.

**MATURE.** Titles rated **M—Mature** have content that may be suitable for persons ages 17 and older. Titles in this category may contain mature sexual themes, more intense violence, and strong language.

**ADULTS ONLY.** Titles rated **AO—Adults Only** have content suitable only for adults. Titles in this category may include graphic depictions of sex and violence. Adult Only products are not intended for persons under the age of 18.

**RATING PENDING.** Titles listed as **RP—Rating Pending** have been submitted to the ESRB and are awaiting final rating.

Using these ratings, which are clearly marked on the outside of the game package, parents should know whether or not the game is appropriate for their child. Unfortunately, the same problem exists with video games as was discussed with television and movie ratings. Parents either do not know about this system or they do not want to know about it. Either the vast majority of parents do not care what their children are playing or they are too afraid of their children's wrath to attempt to enforce the rating system. The same studies that indicate parents do not know what TV shows their kids are watching also show that parents have no idea what video games they are playing.

Why not? Don't they ever stop to watch what their children are playing or ask how the game works? The answer is apparently a resounding "No." Parents cannot blame the game manufacturers. There is a huge market for these games, since they are exciting to the point that many children are actually addicted to them. Manufacturers will not stop creating violent games until parents exert some control over the game content, either by refusing to let their children buy them or by pressuring their governments to put stricter regulations on game content. If parents do not want their children becoming more irritable, angry, aggressive, and even violent because of these games, then they must take the appropriate actions. And to do this, parents must become active, more involved, more aware of what is going on in their children's lives.

## Music

It might seem strange to include a discussion about music in a chapter devoted to television and computer technologies. In recent years, however, the experience of listening to music has undergone a technological transformation that has contributed to the modern parenting crisis.

To be sure, teenage musical tastes have long been a puzzle for parents. The explosion of home music players in the 1940s and 1950s and the ever-increasing wealth of the younger generation made youth a major target of music producers who began to market directly to the younger population. Most people trace the start of the problems between parents and their children's music to the beginning of rock 'n roll in the early 1950s. The explosive entrance on the musical scene of such artists as Elvis Presley, Chuck Berry, and Little Richard was so different from any of the music of previous generations that parents began to worry about the effect that these songs, and their style of delivery, might have on their kids. Research did not back up any of these parental concerns about the early rock music, but then these early songs did not have either offensive language or sexual and violent content.

Unfortunately, all that changed with the popularity of rap music in the 1990s. Suddenly the lyrics became increasingly explicit, particularly in terms of drugs, sex, violence, and even sexual violence. While at first this new type of "music" was considered, like disco, a passing fad, it has proven to have staying power well beyond what most experts and parents would have predicted. It has now been popular among teenagers and their tween siblings for over 10 years and shows no signs of fading out. The popularity of music videos, seen on such television channels as MTV and MuchMusic have added images to the lyrics that make them even more realistic.

Until recently there has not been any research to confirm what most adults were already thinking, that the profanity, sex, and violence in rap music cannot be good for children. A 2003 study, however, demonstrated that violent music lyrics increase aggressive thoughts and feelings. This series of five experiments with over 500 college students clearly showed that violent songs, even humorous ones, increased feelings of hostility without provocation or threat. According to the lead researcher, Dr. Craig Anderson of Iowa State University, the aggressive thoughts and feeling generated by these violent songs have implications for violence in the real world. He concludes:

> Aggressive thoughts can influence perceptions of ongoing social interactions, coloring them with an aggressive tint. Such aggression-biased interpretations can, in turn, instigate a more aggressive response—verbal or physical— than would have been emitted in a nonbiased state, thus provoking an aggressive escalatory spiral of antisocial exchanges.

These results do not mean that every child who listens to rap music will become violent, but there is obviously a tendency for this music to influence those kids who are already troubled through home problems or emotional disturbance. It is clear that there is justification for parental and even governmental restriction of this type of music, as was called for in 1997 by the American Academy of Pediatrics. While it is impossible for parents to completely control what their children are listening to on their disc players or while with friends, they do need to be monitoring what music their kids are buying and restricting what they can play while in the home. This means that parents need to keep up with the various types of popular music, know what the content is, and teach their children what is acceptable and what is not. Otherwise, rather than being a source of pleasure for their youngsters, the music can add to their stress levels by focussing on sex and violence and possibly influencing them into behaviors that are dangerous and illegal.

There is now no question that new technologies are having major effects on young people. While there are definitely positive effects to be derived from television, music, movies, and computer-based technology, there are an equal number of dangers that are creating serious difficulties for our youth. Parents must learn about these dangers and exert controls over their sources to protect their children from stress and potential harm. This is a huge responsibility as many parents find the subject overwhelming. Their children are so enthralled with TV and technology that any parental interference brings waves of protest. Parents are also embarrassed that their children understand how to use the technology better than they do, so they keep away from it. Parents cannot allow themselves to be either bullied by their children or intimidated by their lack of knowledge. They must act by informing themselves of the problems and setting limits that can help their children to avoid them.

# CHAPTER VIII

# The Body

**M**ost of the other issues presented in this book have focused on factors external to children: computers, the education system, parental relationships. But in this final chapter, we turn to the children themselves—their bodies—and examine how the modern parenting crisis is effecting the very physical essence of today's children.

Body image is defined as how people feel about how they look. It is not necessarily based on fact, but rather is psychological in nature. In other words, body image is based on peoples' perceptions of their bodies and the emotions resulting from those perceptions rather than on what actually exists.

Where do those perceptions come from? In large part, they are influenced by media and advertising, which present idealized body images. History shows that stereotypes of what is considered attractive date back for centuries but that the particular beauty ideal has changed with each generation. Prior to 1900, being on the heavy side was highly valued as insurance against tuberculosis. In fact, the

> "Childhood obesity is at epidemic levels in the United States. We have been remiss in shedding light on this problem, which leads to so many other health problems, particularly when we consider the threats this disease imposes on our children. Today we see a nation of young people seriously at risk of starting out obese and dooming themselves to the difficult task of overcoming a tough illness."
>
> **David Satcher, U.S. Surgeon General**

most famous stage actress in the U.S. in the late 1800s, Lillian Russell, weighed over 200 pounds and was idealized for her beauty. A significant shift in this beauty ideal has been occurring since movies and television became popular. Slowly the ideal moved more and more toward thinness. An easy comparison can be made between the body style portrayed in the 1950s by Marilyn Monroe and her compatriots and those of today. The likes of Marilyn's voluptuous curves are no longer seen. By modern standards she might even be considered fat. Instead a review of such popular fan magazines as *People* or *Star* shows that considerably slimmer Paris Hilton or Britney Spears are the bodies of today.

The problem is that the bodies portrayed by movie and television stars and by advertising models are no longer even close to reality. The advertisements generally emphasize tall and thin, while movies and TV emphasize slim waists and large breasts. The statistics confirm the surreal portrait painted by the media. The average American woman is 5'4" tall and weighs 140 pounds. The average American model is 5'11" and weighs 117 pounds. This gives young women a 7 percent chance of being as slim as a catwalk model and only a 1 percent chance of being as thin as a supermodel. This huge difference between real life and fantasy is causing young people, especially girls, to despise their own bodies and to strive to attain a look that is physically impossible for all but a small percentage of them.

Strangely, at the same time that the media offers these idealized images of physical beauty and health, they fill their programs and publications with advertisements of junk food and other unhealthy fare. Add to the equation the marketing of alcohol and tobacco products, and one finds a rather bizarre contradiction: children are encouraged to emulate celebrities who are skinny and healthy, while being enticed to buy food that will make them fat and unhealthy. Then, throw in the actions and reactions of parents, who seem just as confused by the jumble of media messages being thrown their way and who are doing a poor job of helping their children to make sense of it all. It is no wonder that children have body image problems!

## Thinness

The dissatisfaction with their bodies causes a huge number of young girls (and even older women for that matter) to strive for thinness. The number one wish for girls ages 11 to 17 is to be thinner. Even very young children are being affected by the thinness ideal. A 1991 study showed that 42 percent of children in Grade 1 to 3 wanted to be thinner. Another study, also from 1991 showed that 81 percent of ten-year-old girls were afraid of becoming fat. The power of these media portrayals of young women is so great that, in 1999, the American Academy of Pediatrics found that 47 percent of the subject girls were influenced, by magazine pictures, to lose weight, but only 29 percent of them actually were overweight.

The drive for the thin ideal is placing incredible stress on those who do not conform—or who perceive themselves as not conforming. Psychologically, an obsession with a thin body image can cause insecurity and low self-esteem. These feelings can be severe enough as to make many young people unable to enjoy their formative years. Physically, the stress can lead to eating disorders. Before

"Dear Diary:

I was looking at my *Seventeen* magazine today, (it took me about an hour to finish) and I caught myself feeling absolutely miserable about myself looking at the poems. I flip the glossy pages looking at beautiful women. People I want to be. I learn make-up tips and read articles all judging me, telling me who I am, who I want to be. I'm angry and depressed as I close the magazine and place it by my side. I hate it. I never hated anything more. But I still read it. I still subscribe. I still can't wait for another issue to arrive in my mailbox and I won't stop ... Until I'm perfect.

14-year-old girl

**Source: www.mediawatch.com**

the 1970s, eating disorders were rare. Today they are an increasing reality among children, especially girls. Recent statistics suggest that about 1 percent of adolescent girls have Anorexia Nervosa, while about 4 percent are bulimic. While these are not huge numbers, the alarming fact is that they are on the rise, despite the knowledge that now exists about them. These are incredibly powerful diseases that develop subtly so that parents often do not notice the initial signs. Once they are entrenched, even trained therapists have great difficulty treating these problems. Eating disorders not only can create tremendous stress for the sufferer and in fact, the entire family, but they can actually be deadly. This is far too high a price to pay for an artificially created ideal.

## Steroids

While girls are the main victims of the distorted body images portrayed in the media, boys do not go unscathed. While they are only rarely afflicted by the thinness craze, they are effected by the muscular image that the media present for them. The same insecurity that effects females as a result of not being thin enough strikes many males who feel that they are too skinny. As a result there has been a major increase in obsessive and often unsupervised weight training and the use of anabolic steroids and dietary supplements to help these young males "bulk up." *Anabolic* means "building body tissue." Anabolic steroids help build muscle tissue and increase body mass by acting like the body's natural male hormone, testosterone. Whether they are called 'roids, juice, hype, or pump, anabolic steroids are powerful drugs that many people take in high doses to boost athletic performance.

While much is now known about the serious effects of eating disorders, few parents are aware of the equally serious side effects of steroid use. These effects are not just on the body, but include psychological consequences as well. The table below summarizes the problems that steroid use can cause.

## Physical Effects

- High blood pressure and instances of heart disease
- Liver damage and cancers
- Stroke and blood clots
- Urinary and bowel problems, such as diarrhea
- Headaches, aching joints and muscle cramps
- Nausea and vomiting
- Sleep problems
- Increased risk of ligament and tendon injuries
- Severe acne, especially on face and back
- Baldness

## Psychological Effects

- "Roid rage"—severe, aggressive behavior that may result in violence, such as fighting or destroying property
- Severe mood swings
- Hallucinations—seeing or hearing things that are not really there
- Paranoia—extreme feelings of mistrust and fear
- Anxiety and panic attacks
- Depression and thoughts of suicide
- Anger, hostility, and irritability

**Source: American Academy of Pediatrics**

As this table indicates, the possible consequences of trying to speed up nature's processes through drug use can be very severe. The availability and widespread use of these drugs is becoming better known from all the media attention focusing on steroid use in professional athletics, including the Olympics. Few of the stories, however, have discussed the possible side effects of these drugs in any detail. Often no symptoms appear for several years, only to erupt dramatically. For example, at least 25 professional wrestlers have died since 1997 from heart attacks, despite the fact that they are relatively young and in excellent physical condition. Steroid use is suspected in most of these deaths. Besides the dangers of steroid use itself is the fact that they cannot usually be obtained legally and must then be bought on the "black market." As a result the quality of the drugs cannot be guaranteed and they may contain almost anything. If a steroid is contaminated with impurities, this can damage internal organs or cause cancer, life-threatening infections (especially if injected), and death. Since many of these steroids are injected, those who share needles may get AIDS, hepatitis B and C, and bacterial endocarditis (a frequently fatal infection of the heart valves). This litany of possible negative effects of trying to match the muscular images delivered by the media seems far too dangerous for the potential results.

If their adolescents have developed a serious interest in body-building, parents need to be aware of the dangers of both unsupervised training and of steroid or supplement use. Done properly, bodybuilding is a very healthy activity. It is up to the parents to see that it is being done under the supervision of a professional trainer and that no artificial means are being used to speed up the development of the muscles.

Whether it is their daughter's obsession with thinness or their son's obsession with being "ripped," parents must be aware of the messages their children are receiving through their friends and the media. How to do this involves many of the things discussed in the previous chapter: becoming familiar with the media and the technologies their children are using, monitoring the kinds of content their children are reading and absorbing, and most important, communicating with their children. Having face-to-face conversations about these issues, where parents can talk with their children about the images the media are presenting and the blueprints their heredity has given them, can do wonders for opening up a child's mind.

## Obesity

At the other end of the weight scale from those children trying to compete with images of thinness are those children whose bodies seem to have given up the fight altogether. Obesity, or the abnormal accumulation of body fat, has been identified as a growing problem for modern youth and poses as many health and social risks for children as does the thinness and steroid problems.

Obesity in children has the distinction of being both a symptom of a problem and a problem itself. As a symptom, obesity in a child could indicate hormonal difficulties, a poor diet, a lack of exercise, or a combination of these. As a problem, obesity can lead to health difficulties, self-esteem concerns, and being the target of teasing and bullying. Either way, obesity in children is a potential stressor that will make the lives of these children more difficult than if they were of an average weight. It is essential, therefore, that parents understand the scope of childhood obesity and the roles they play in both causing and solving this problem.

## The Scope of Childhood Obesity

The scope of the childhood obesity problem in developed countries worldwide is difficult to measure because of definitions that differ slightly and a confusion of terms. For example, the term "overweight" may tend to mean a milder degree of excess fat than "obesity," but the cut-off point for each label depends on how you measure a body in the first place. For example, the U.S. National Institute of Health defines obesity as being more than 20 percent above ideal body weight (approximately 20 percent for males and 30 percent for females). The Body-Mass Index or BMI, offers a slightly more precise definition, through the following formula:

$$BMI = \left( \frac{\text{Weight in Pounds}}{\text{Height in Inches} \times \text{Height in Inches}} \right) \times 703$$

Any BMI of 30 or over is considered by most definitions to be obese, while a BMI over 25 is considered to be overweight. However one defines obesity, there is general agreement that children's weight problems are becoming more common, although the exact numbers depend on who you ask.

**Statistic**   More than 15 percent of children and adolescents in the United States are overweight. This figure has doubled in the past 2 decades.

**National Center for Health Statistics in the United States, (1999-2002)**

**Statistic**  More than 25 percent of children age 6 to 11 are obese. Among children age 12 to 17, 25 percent of girls and 18 percent of boys are obese. The number of overweight children 6-17 years of age was found to have doubled in the last 30 years.
**University of Michigan Health System, 2004**

**Statistic**  37 percent of Canadian children between the ages of 2–11 are overweight, of which 18 percent are considered to be obese.
**Canadian Heart and Stroke Foundation, 2001**

No matter which set of figures is used, these numbers are very high. Worse, they are continuing to rise. Parents need to be very concerned about this problem, as the consequences of childhood obesity can be extremely serious.

## The Consequences of Childhood Obesity

### Diabetes

One of the first trends that has been noticed by the medical profession is the rapid increase in type 2 diabetes. This illness, which comprises over 90 percent of all diabetes sufferers, was once only found in adults, but now is being diagnosed much more frequently in children. While statistics on this frequency are still being gathered, clinics all across Canada and the United States are noticing an increase in the incidence of type 2 diabetes in young people under 20 years of age.

In a normally functioning body, cells use blood glucose as their basic fuel. To help the blood sugar pass into the cells and use the sugar effectively, the body produces insulin.

**Surge in Childhood Diabetes**

• Between 8 and 45 percent of newly diagnosed cases of childhood diabetes are type 2, associated with obesity.
• Whereas 4 percent of childhood diabetes was type 2 in 1990, that number has risen to approximately 20 percent
• Of children diagnosed with Type 2 diabetes, 85 percent are obese

**Wellness International Network Ltd - www.winltd.com**

In people with diabetes, blood glucose (sugar) levels are too high, because glucose remains in the blood rather than entering cells. There are two reasons this can happen, accounting for the two main types of diabetes. People with the type 1 variety do not produce any insulin because of damage to the islet cells in the pancreas. These people must take regular insulin shots to keep their blood glucose levels down. People with type 2 diabetes usually have two problems, however: they do not make quite enough insulin and the cells of their bodies do not seem to take in glucose as eagerly as they should in the body. When glucose builds up in the blood instead of going into cells, the cells become starved for energy, resulting in a variety of very noticeable and debilitating symptoms (see sidebar). Left untreated, diabetes can lead to blindness, leg amputations, kidney disease, heart attack, and stroke.

> **Symptoms of Diabetes**
> - Frequent thirst
> - Frequent urination
> - Constant hunger
> - Weight loss
> - Fatigue
> - Blurred vision
> - Depression, lack of energy or irritability
> - Noticeable behavioral changes
> - Nausea or stomach pain
> - Frequent infections or sores that are slow to heal

The cause of type 2 diabetes is not precisely known but it appears to be related to increased weight gain rather than to the autoimmune pancreatic islet cell damage that causes type 1 diabetes. Most individuals diagnosed with type 2 diabetes are significantly overweight with a Body Mass Index greater than the 85th percentile (for 5-year-olds this equates to a BMI of 17, while for 17 year-olds it is a BMI of 25). Sedentary lifestyle and poor dietary habits, combined with the genetic predisposition of certain ethnic groups, are the most likely reasons that there is now a virtual epidemic of this form of diabetes. Type 2 diabetes can be controlled through diet, exercise, and drugs, and children who contract it can lead relatively normal lives, but it does change the way they live and it can become harder and harder to control later in life. Since it is highly preventable merely by maintaining average weight, parents must pay careful attention to their children's weight development.

## Future Heart Disease

An increasing volume of research on obese children is showing that they are at much higher risk than normal-weight children of future heart problems. A study by Dr. Kam Woo at the Chinese University of Hong Kong showed that overweight pre-teens tend to have the thick, stiff arteries of a 45-year-old smoker. This research led to the prediction that by adulthood, these obese children would have a 3 to 5 times greater risk of having a heart attack or stroke than their normal-weight compatriots. Of even greater concern is a recent finding that the damage done to arteries in childhood is not reversible by improved heart-health behavior later in life. Studies published in the *Journal of the American Medical Association* showed that the fatty plaque that builds up in the arteries as a result of poor diet and lack of exercise leaves some sort of mark on them that cannot be reversed. The only answer at present would appear to be prevention of this fatty build-up in childhood.

Associated research to these arterial studies also shows that the blood pressure of children and adolescents has been rising over the past decade, largely due to a greater tendency to be overweight. High blood pressure (hypertension) is a condition that is often without symptoms and may lead to heart attack, heart failure, stroke, kidney failure, dementia, visual impairment, and premature death. When the cause of hypertension is unknown — as it is in the vast majority of cases — the condition is called primary, or essential, hypertension. It seems clear that being overweight contributes to this problem, but the exact mechanism is not yet known.

Another indicator of the potential effects of obesity on the heart and arteries is the presence of what is known in the medical profession as "metabolic syndrome." Metabolic syndrome is defined as the presence of 3 or more out of 5 key risk factors for heart disease and stroke in an individual. People with metabolic syndrome are at an increased risk of heart disease, stroke, or type 2 diabetes. These risk factors in adults are:

- Abdominal obesity: waist circumference greater than 102 cm (40 inches) for men, greater than 88 cm (35 inches) for women.

- Elevated levels of triglycerides (blood fats)

- Low levels of high density lipoprotein cholesterol (HDL or good cholesterol)

- High blood pressure (greater than 135/85)

- Insulin resistance or glucose intolerance

A study in the *New England Journal of Medicine* in 2004 found that the prevalence of metabolic syndrome was high among obese people and increased with the severity of their obesity. This means that the early signs of potential heart attacks and strokes are presented in young children and become more severe with the increasing weight of the child.

Obviously there is ample evidence that childhood obesity greatly increases the chances of heart or stroke problems later in life. Since it is possible that the damage done by being overweight as a child cannot be reversed, then the only answer is to try to prevent the problem in the first place.

## Asthma

Researchers in both the United States and Great Britain have clearly shown a relationship between obesity and asthma. Since 1980, the number of cases of asthma in children has risen over 160 percent and the disease now effects approximately 5 million children in the United States. In addition to asthma, scientists have also seen a higher incidence of obesity in children of Western cultures. According to a 2001 study in the journal *Thorax*, excess weight may predispose children to the development of asthma. The results of the study showed that the prevalence of asthma was as much as 73 percent higher in children with the highest BMI, compared with children of normal weight. Another study, conducted by Dr. Carlos A. Camargo, Jr., of Brigham and Woman's Hospital in Boston, concluded that the most overweight children had approximately twice the risk of asthma compared with the thinnest boys, and the most overweight girls had 1.5 times the risk of asthma compared to the thinnest children.

The exact relationship between obesity and asthma is not yet known. There may be a genetic link between the two, or it could be that being overweight puts more strain on the airways and causes them to inflame more easily. No matter what the cause it seems clear that being obese carries a greater danger of contracting asthma, which is just one more reason to help children maintain a normal weight.

## Depression

Being overweight or worse, being obese, can often lead to negative feelings about one's own body, which in turn negatively affects a person's mental condition. Negative body image is linked to depression, low self-esteem, lowered sexual drive, and poor health habits. Most obese individuals feel ostracized by society in which they live. They are teased, bullied, and made to feel inferior by the svelte body images projected in the media. Overweight people find that even the medical profession is negative towards them as these professionals tend to feel that the condition is self-afflicted and perhaps less acceptable than other medical conditions.

Unfortunately, obesity carries an undeserved social stigma in our society. The obese are often stereotyped as stupid and lazy. Some researchers have even found that those who were obese achieved less education and lower income and that fewer married. A recent study by Latner and Stunkard has shown that the stigma of obesity, already severe in 1960, has increased measurably more than 4 decades later. Facing this negative social image from an early age takes its toll on overweight children and forces them to learn adaptive strategies. The lucky ones learn to laugh at their condition along with their tormentors, developing the "jolly fat man" approach. Less fortunate children are forced to withdraw from their peers, often resulting in serious depression.

It seems that the relationship between depression and obesity is even more complicated than it appears. Apparently, while obesity causes depression in many cases there is also evidence that depression can influence obesity. In other words, depressed people can become obese as a result of their depression. According to Johns Hopkins University, research has found that an amino acid, tryptophan, increases in the blood when carbohydrates are eaten. Carbohydrates stimulate the secretion of insulin, which speeds the uptake of tryptophan into the central nervous system, where it is converted into serotonin in the brain. Serotonin is the neurotransmitter that, when not in sufficient supply in the brain, results in depression. Patients with carbohydrate cravings are thought to have a faulty serotonin feedback mechanism that neglects to tell the body to stop craving carbohydrates. The more carbohydrates that are eaten, the better these people feel psychologically, so they continue to eat.

This result of this problem is a "vicious circle." As the person eats to feel less depressed, he or she becomes overweight. As the weight increases, the person becomes depressed by the increasingly negative body image. To alleviate this depression the person eats more, and the cycle continues. It is often hard to tell which comes first, the obesity or the depression. This can be confusing to parents and often professional intervention may be required to sort out the cause of the problem. It may be that, in addition to diet control and an exercise program, anti-depressants may be required to solve the weight problem.

Of further concern to parents of obese children is a recent link found between people who are depressed and obese and the possibility of future heart disease. In a recent issue of *Brain, Behavior, and*

*Immunity*, the official journal of the tongue-twisting Psychoneuro-immunology Research Society, it was discovered that obesity and depression may work together to cause the chronic low-level inflammation associated with atherosclerosis and increased risk of heart disease. This seems like adding insult to injury, as being over-weight and depressed is bad enough. Nevertheless this link appar-ently exists and is just one more reason to avoid obesity.

It seems probable that, in our fast-food, low-exercise society, the majority of overweight children are depressed because of their weight, and not overweight due to their depression. But because this cannot be assumed, parents need to be careful how they deal with their children's weight problems. If signs of depression are noted at an early age, immediate professional intervention should be sought before obesity becomes a problem. If no signs of depres-sion are present, then the solution is likely to be diet and exercise and parents can proceed accordingly. If parents are not sure which came first, they should obtain the advice of a medical doctor or a psychologist before attempting any treatment.

## Bullying

It was mentioned above that because of modern society's stigma against being overweight, overweight children are often teased and bullied. In fact, overweight children are up to 4 times more likely than normal-weight children to be punched, kicked, teased, shoved around, and left out of groups. Of even more concern was the find-ing that obese girls are even more likely to be bullied than boys are. These are very serious, if not unexpected, findings especially in the light of the alarming attention that bullying has received since the 1999 Columbine affair.

Children who are bullied suffer massive damage to their self-esteem because, despite the fact that only a relatively small percent-age of children are bullies, their victims feel that everyone is against them. This is the result of the fact that the majority of children are either afraid to intervene in defense of the victims of bullying or they are unsure what to do. This makes them do nothing, which is seen by the victim as support for the bully. In reality, most children do not like to witness bullying and do not agree with it; they just do not know what to do about it.

A further result of the above research is more surprising. It was found that many overweight and obese 15- and 16-year-old boys become bullies themselves out of the frustration of being bullied for so many years. Often these students are larger than their compatriots and find that they can retaliate for their years of suffering by becoming exactly what they have hated for so long. This reaction is understandable because it means that, instead of being helpless in the face of torment, the overweight child can actually take action. Unfortunately these actions are not necessarily against those who have bullied them but towards other weak children in the population.

Bullying has become a huge problem in today's society and it is clear that overweight and obese children suffer the most. While it is important to act against bullying, through education and the imposition of consequences, it seems even more important for parents to prevent their children from being such obvious bully targets in the first place.

## The Causes of Childhood Obesity

A society such as ours would appear to have little need to be told what is causing obesity. The massive emphasis placed on being slim by the media has made it common knowledge that eating too much and exercising too little is the problem. The answer is obviously to eat less and exercise more. Unfortunately it is not that simple. Changes in society's values and ways of living have made this simple plan very difficult to implement. If the epidemic of childhood obesity is to be eliminated, then parents need to understand what these changes are and then take the necessary steps to eliminate the problems as childhood obesity is too serious a problem to ignore.

## 10 Ways to Tell if Your Child Has a Weight Problem

While these suggestions may seem obvious, far too many parents either refuse to believe that their child has a problem, or they wait too long to address it.

1. Her doctor tells you so.

2. Your child complains about being teased about his size.

3. Your child's clothes seem to get too small too fast.

4. Shopping for clothes with your child is a nightmare.

5. Your child refuses to be seen in a bathing suit.

6. Your child's friendships are suddenly changing.

7. Your child withdraws from activities he previously enjoyed.

8. You find yourself referring to her as "big-boned" or "large."

9. You notice your child huffing and puffing after a simple task such as climbing of stairs.

10. Your child tells you she thinks she is overweight.

While weight gain can occur at any time, many parents don't address the issue until it becomes a much **bigger** problem. When you wait until it's a problem of larger proportions, it's harder to treat.

**Source: *The Can-Do Eating Plan for Overweight Kids and Teens* by Michelle Daum, MS, RD**

## Diet

Several factors have reshaped dietary habits in developed countries. First is the decline of breakfast. Nutritionists have proven over and over again that eating a good breakfast is a key component of good nutrition. A solid foundation from which to start the day helps to prevent children from snacking and overeating during the rest of the day. The problem, however, is time. When both parents are hurrying off to work, often before their children are up or at least before they have eaten, then the children often skip breakfast. They may not feel particularly hungry and they may have a time crunch themselves. Children are generally not as well organized as their parents and unless something is prepared for them, they either will grab snack food or not eat at all. Still, it is vital that children eat a good breakfast and if they need to be supervised for this to happen, then that's what parents must do. It does not take long to make a bowl of oatmeal or to scramble some eggs. It also does not take long to eat it. It just requires that parents insist, from an early age, that breakfast be eaten daily so as to ensure a healthy start to the day.

Lunchtime eating has also changed in recent years. Many parents no longer make lunches for their children. Far too often children are given money and told to buy their lunch. While school cafeterias do offer relatively nutritious meals, most children choose to buy snack food at the nearest convenience store. This usually consists of carbonated beverages, which are almost 50 percent sugar, and packaged foods that are loaded with fat. Once again the time factor rears its ugly head as the reason behind this trend. Parents just do not have the time and energy to buy lunch food and prepare the lunches daily so they throw money at the problem and pretend that they do not know what their kids are buying with it.

It may be a fact that some kids will throw away all or part of their prepared lunch on occasion, but the majority of kids eat most of what is given to them. If parents consult with their children as to what they want in the lunches, then the chances are good that they will eat them. Parents also need to ensure that their children don't have large amounts of money to spend on junk food, so that they will not be tempted to dispose of their lunch every day. Since peer pressure is an important factor in adolescent lives, it is vital that students eat their lunches in the cafeterias so that the majority of kids are not buying their food outside the school. If most of the students are eating in, then the rest will follow. Unfortunately this is not presently the case.

Finally, our society has seen the virtual elimination of the family dinner. Where once the entire family sat down together each evening to eat a common meal, now the majority of households either eat out or each family member throws something together for themselves. This relatively new tendency has resulted from the hectic world that most families now inhabit. With both parents working, often for long hours, no parent is available to prepare the dinners. When parents do arrive home they are confronted with an array of family commitments: sports practices, music lessons, dance classes, and so forth. Parents are literally greeting each other briefly as they pass in the hallways on their way to driving their kids to these appointments. There simply is no time for a sit-down meal, so each person snatches what he or she can.

What parents and children, alike, actually snatch is usually some sort of prepared food that is high in fat and low in nutrition, like a hamburger or a bag of potato chips. When a parent prepares a meal the chances are that it will be balanced for food groups and relatively low in fat content. Fast food and snacks, on the other hand, are not balanced at all. Nutrition is not the only thing that is neglected when families do not eat together. They also lose the chance for family communication. The family dinner is an important component of family life that has become neglected in the interests of work and structured activities.

To suggest that families cut out junk food at breakfast, lunch, and dinner seems obvious enough, but it is not easy given the incredible marketing push of junk food companies. Pepsi-Cola, for example, spends about $2 billion a year on advertising while McDonald's spends around $1.2 billion. These are huge dollar amounts, and they are well spent, from the perspective of the food companies. Americans spent about $110 billion on fast food alone in 2001 and drank about 600 cans of pop per person. According to the University of Washington's Teen Health and the Media web site, the average child watches 10,000 food advertisements a year on television, of which only 2 percent are for fruits, vegetables, or beans. Ads for junk food are found in magazines, in product placements in the movies, in stores, on the Internet, and even in schools.

Junk food advertising is being particularly hard on young girls. By making these foods glamorous and attractive, they are competing with ads and programs in the same media that portray women as ultra thin and chic. This creates confusion and can lead to the bingeing and purging cycle that is found in bulimia. At the very least it creates stress and worry in these young ladies as they quaff their Cokes and munch their fries while worrying about weight gain.

To counter the influences of the junk food media, therefore, it is important that parents set a good nutritional example for their kids. They should not eat out, especially in fast food "restaurants," except as a rare treat. They should not buy copious quantities of junk food and eat this while watching television. In fact they should not have junk food in the home at all. Instead parents should eat fruits and vegetables and drink juices and encourage their children to do the same. The example parents set combined with their determination that their children will eat proper meals, will go far in solving the present obesity problem.

## Play

Few aspects of children's lives have changed as dramatically in the past 20 years as their play habits. Where once playgrounds and schoolyards were full of children playing made-up games or engaged in unsupervised sporting activities such as "scrub" baseball or touch football outside of school hours, now these same playgrounds are almost empty. Research evidence also points to a decline in unstructured children's play. Studies by the University of Michigan's Survey Research Center indicate that since the 1970s children have lost 12 hours per week in free time, which includes a 25 percent drop in play and a 50 percent drop in unstructured outdoor activities. Similarly, Dr. Lisa Sutherland of the University of North Carolina at Chapel Hill shows that children are 13 percent less physically active than they were in the 1980s. Most of this activity loss is from a lack of unstructured play.

How did playtime disappear? In many ways, the decline in children's play time parallels the decline in adult leisure time; in both cases, unstructured activities without practical ends have been replaced by structured ones with practical importance. In the adult work world people waste as little time as possible, they equate their work with who they are, and they put a premium on speed. Efficiency is valued and wasting time is not. This is not a healthy attitude for adults because it creates much stress in the work world, but it is a particularly devastating philosophy when applied to children. Under this line of reasoning, unstructured play activities are considered to be a waste of time so they are replaced with structured ones. Free play turns into dance lessons, music lessons, and organized sports.

Furthermore, in this affluent society most parents can now afford these activities, so they pile them on to make their children as efficient and well-rounded as possible. Of course these parents mean well, and they really do want the best for their children. They just do not see that their speed-and-efficiency model of work fits their children even less than it fits their own situations. Children are not yet ready for this adult philosophy, yet they are plunged into it because it is thought to be good for them. It isn't.

This over-structuring of children's activities may be exposing them to many positive influences, but it is also having negative effects on the stress levels and on their bodies. Few activities are as efficient in burning calories as daily free play. The average 75-pound child will burn 260 calories in just 45 minutes of free play, or the equivalent of a large cookie and a soft drink. The same cannot be said for even organized sports as practices are rarely daily and usually consist of periods of instruction and periodic drills. While this does not mean that children should not be involved in structured activities, it does mean that a balance needs to be maintained so that as much time as possible is allowed for free play.

It is not just sports and lessons that are now being structured by parents, even the free play time is being programmed. Children no longer are allowed to simply drift over to the playground in their free time and see who is there; they must have "play dates." For the few parents who are uninitiated to this new form of activity, play dates are when parents call up other parents and make arrangements for their children to play together. This usually involves a certain amount of parental supervision as once a date is made the kids cannot be expected to find their own activities. Instead the parents take them to a show, a swimming pool, or some other semi-structured activity. Never mind whether that's who the child wants to play with or what he or she wants to do. Certainly some physical activity is involved in these dates, but nowhere near what would be occurring in totally unstructured play.

> John Borst writing in The Social Edge.com in April 2002, wondered where we are leaving space for young children to just move at their own rhythm, to just play in the outdoors in such places as a backyard, sandbox, a vacant lot, the street, or if they are really fortunate, a forest or nearby valley stream? He goes on to say "In this noisy adult world, do we ever allow them quiet time to live in their imaginations?"

Part of the reasoning behind parents' objections to unstructured play has to do with their fear that the child will be molested or abducted. While these crimes do occasionally occur, parents should not live in fear of them because they are relatively rare. They probably seem more frequent than they actually are due to the massive amount of publicity that surrounds each event. Certainly parents should be vigilant and know where their children are, but it is not necessary to structure their children's entire lives just because of the remote possibility of abduction. Dr. Claire LeBlanc, chairwoman of the Canadian Pediatric Society committee on healthy living and activity, says that, "In the vast majority of cases (of fears of abduction), they're overreactions."

Another aspect of parents' fears for their children's safety is the tendency to drive their children everywhere. The long lines of cars dropping their kids off at school in the morning and picking them up afterwards gives dramatic testimony to this tendency. Walking or biking to school burns off many surplus calories and also gives the children time to socialize and play with each other. If children have been properly "street proofed" by their parents, they will not accept rides with strangers. If they are taught to go in small groups, then strangers will not attempt to pick them up. Certainly some precautions are necessary, but driving children everywhere does them no favors, either mentally or physically. In fact, it hurts them.

A 2003 study funded by the Canadian Population Health Initiative and led by Dr. Mark Tremblay at the University of Saskatchewan found that unorganized physical activity was more protective against obesity than organized sport because it tended to be more frequent, was undertaken for a longer amount of time, and goes further toward developing a lifelong appreciation of physical activity.

Children need as much unstructured playtime as possible for both their intellectual development and their physical well-being. This is no longer happening for all the wrong reasons. The playgrounds, vacant lots, and even the streets need to be full of children playing made-up games. The ball diamonds, undeveloped lots, and tennis courts need to be used by kids playing sports with their own rules and no coaches. Two girls can play tennis with two old racquets and a scruffy ball borrowed from the dog. Three boys can play 500 with just a ball and a bat. Four can play touch football, each pretending they are NFL stars. The list is endless as are the possibilities to burn calories. The modern trend to structure and organization needs to be reversed as soon as possible.

## TV and Video Games

This subject was well covered in the Media and Technology chapter but the effect of these activities on obesity must be mentioned.

The University of Saskatchewan study mentioned in the previous sidebar also found that children who watch more than 3 hours of television a day are 50 percent more likely to be obese than children who watch fewer than 2 hours. And television is probably the lesser of the two offenders. Even more dangerous for fitness are the use of chat lines by girls and video games by boys (with some crossover of course). At one time, children who were bored after school would ride their bicycles or go for walks. Now they plunk themselves down in front of the TV or computer screen and exercise only their fingers—for 38 hours a week.

Why do parents allow such an obviously mentally and physically unhealthy behavior to occur? Generally parents are either too busy to impose controls or they are too afraid of their children's reaction if they do. If no one is home after school, it is extremely hard to set limits on television watching and video playing. If parents do not bother to check on what their children are doing in their rooms, then they won't know how long they are spending on these activities. If they find that the TV is an excellent babysitter, then they will leave their small children in front of it for hours. If they are too tired or stressed to enforce their will or too confused about how to set rules and give consequences for breaking them, then they will simply allow their children to do what they want. This is what is presently happening and this is a major reason why the children are getting heavier.

## Parental Example

Few parents appear to understand how important it is to set a good example for their children. Youngsters love their parents and, especially in the early years, tend to want to be like them. This is as true in the area of physical activity as it is in moral development. In 2003 Statistics Canada found that children tend to mirror their parents when it comes to lifestyle choices. Daughters of obese parents were 6 times more likely to be obese while sons' chances of obesity were 3 times higher than children from average weight parents. Of course heredity plays a part and there are certainly inherited hormonal conditions that will cause obesity. The study showed, however, that where parents were inactive, children were inactive as well. If the parents did not eat fruits and vegetables, then neither did their children. If the parents smoked, then their children were more likely to do the same. In other words, the children were following their parents' example in a majority of the cases.

If parents do not want their children to be obese or even over-weight, they must set the example by following a physically active and nutritionally sound lifestyle. When the kids are young, week-end activities should include hiking, biking, skating, or swimming. Meals should be eaten at the table as a family and should include home-made food that is nutritionally balanced. Parents who do not want their children to smoke should not smoke themselves. The old saying "Do as I say, not as I do" will not work on children; if something is alright for their parents, whom they love and admire, then it must be alright for them too.

## Educational Failings

Even the public education system is not doing enough to help solve the growing obesity problem. While they do offer nutritional advice in Health or Physical education classes, they are not doing nearly enough to promote active lifestyles. Few school systems have daily physical education classes, and even the classes that do exist tend to promote team sports rather than healthy lifestyles. Even worse, the increased emphasis on standardized testing has resulted in about 40 percent of American schools eliminating recess. Atlanta, Georgia, is even starting to build schools without play-grounds. The opportunity for 15 minutes of play and unstructured activity twice a day is being lost, as is the chance of a mental break from academic endeavors. Educators should, and probably do, know better. They are simply responding to parental pressure to increase academic content and eliminate "frivolous" unstructured activities. They need to arm themselves with the growing body of research on the physical and mental benefits of play and face their well-meaning but misinformed parents with these facts. If they don't, they are not only not doing their job, but they are harming their students.

## Alcohol, Tobacco and Junk Food

The final issue with body image concerns the marketing of alcohol and tobacco to youth. Most parents would probably agree that these products are not desirable for their children. Nevertheless, because parents have lost (or abandoned) their ability to provide guidance about the dangers of alcohol and tobacco, many children now use them.

Underage drinking is a huge problem among teenagers, yet companies are allowed to advertise in magazines and on television where children can easily view them. One study by Georgetown University's Center for Alcohol Marketing and Youth showed that both boys and girls were more likely to see alcohol magazine ads than adults. The study also showed that girls were much more likely than boys to be overexposed to alcohol advertising in magazines, probably because they tend to read magazines that show movie stars and the glitterati more than boys do.

A classic example of alcohol advertising that easily reaches many teenagers is that shown during the Super Bowl. In 2003, Anheuser-Busch, the manufacturers of Budweiser beer, spent $20 million on 11 commercials. These are extremely clever ads that make it seem cool to drink beer. While hard liquor advertisements are not allowed on major network television or on any Canadian networks, they do appear on cable TV, which is an integral part of many homes. Once again these very slick commercials make it seem like drinking is fun and harmless and that everyone is doing it. Teenagers are particularly susceptible to these marketing pitches because of their relative naiveté, their risk-taking tendencies, and overall feelings of invulnerability. Like adults, they often find that alcohol temporarily reduces their stress, which also adds to its attractiveness.

Although tobacco advertisements are prohibited from television, they are allowed to advertise in American magazines and to sponsor sporting events in the United States. While similar activities are banned in Canada, American magazines are readily available on the newsstands, and sporting events, such as car racing, are seen on American television channels. Despite solid scientific evidence that tobacco products kill hundreds of thousands of people in Canada and the United States every year, the major producers are still targeting the teenage market. And it's working! In spite of educational campaigns to the contrary, teenage smoking, especially among girls, is on the rise. A major drawing card for teenage girls is that they believe cigarettes will help control weight gain. Nicotine is also a well-known stress reducer, at least on a temporary basis, and therefore becomes attractive to stressed-out teens of both sexes.

> "Today, teenage girls smoke in record numbers, because the tobacco companies have been successful in associating smoking with independence, freedom, rebellion, and for many girls, a key for weight loss."
>
> **Matthew Myers, President of Campaign for Tobacco Free Kids**
>
> **Quoted by Christy Feig, CNN Medical Unit, March 27, 2001**

Advertising of dangerous products like alcohol and tobacco needs to be restricted by governments and countered through educational programs and parental counseling. Children do not need to be taught that these products are good for them by slick media productions. Parents must take a leadership role within their own families and teach their children about the dangers of these products. The alternative—being silent and letting children find out about these products on their own—at best creates stress and confusion in young minds about what is right and wrong. At worst, the silence can kill them.

Over the past 20 years a number of lifestyle changes have occurred that changed our children's lives. The hard-working, hurry-up lifestyle that most adults are following has filtered down to our children so that they are no longer allowed to play freely as they once did. Diets have changed for the worse with fewer families eating dinner together and more families having crowded timetables. Both parents' working has meant that more children are unsupervised after school, giving them too much time to play the very attractive and addictive video games and watch the highly entertaining movies on television. The result is a rapidly growing population, but growing in the waistline rather than in numbers. Obesity not only hurts children physically, especially in future years, it also harms them mentally as they are teased and abused by their peers. To change this situation will mean massive lifestyle changes for parents, but these changes will be good for them as well. Parents who care about their children need to make these changes so that the next generation is not stressed out and overweight. This is no legacy for parents to leave.

# Selected
# Bibliography

The body of research on youth stress and the parenting crisis has been growing over the past decade. Academic researchers, professional therapists, educators, and even the media have sought to understand the causes and solutions to these problems. This book drew heavily from this growing research. The following list provides a full citation both to those sources directly referred to in the text and to those sources not quoted directly.

All Internet web sites were current as of 1 April 2005, except where noted.

## Chapter 1

Bradley, Kristen. "Survey shows high levels of teen stress." 16 Oct 2002. *International Child And Youth Care Network*. [http://www.cyc-net.org/today2002/today021016.html].

Centers for Disease Control. 2002. "Youth Risk Behavior Surveillance – United States 2001." MMRW 2002: 51(SS-04) 1-64.

Centre for Addiction and Mental Health. *Ontario Student Drug Use Survey*. Toronto: 2003.

Centers for Disease Control. *Tobacco Use among Middle and High School Students—United States, 2002*. Atlanta: 2002.

Colman, Adrian. "Teenage Depression." *Youth Studies Australia* (September 2003).

Cunningham, Alison. "Adolescent Female Aggression: Proposal for a Research Agenda." Paper presented at the Annual Convention of the Canadian Psychological Association, Ottawa. 2000.

Currie, Candace, et al., eds. "Young People's Health in Context." *Health Behaviour in School-aged Children (HBSC) Study: International Report from the 2001/2002 Survey.* 2004. Geneva: World Health Organization, 2004. [http://www.euro.who.int/Document/e82923.pdf].

Dallman, Mary F., et al. "Chronic Stress and Obesity: A New View of 'Comfort Food.'" *Proceedings of the National Academy of Sciences* 100 (2003): 11696-701.

DeVoe, J.F., et al. *Indicators of School Crime and Safety: 2002.* U.S. Departments of Education and Justice. NCES 2003–009/NCJ 196753. Washington, DC: 2002.

Foshee, V.A., et al. "The Safe Dates Project: Theoretical Basis, Evaluation Design, and Selected Baseline Findings. Youth Violence Prevention: Description and baseline data from 13 evaluation projects." In K. Powell and D. Hawkins (Eds.). *American Journal of Preventive Medicine* Supplement, 12, no. 5 (1996): 39-47.

"Girls aged 11-15 more likely to smoke." 30 March 2004. *National Statistics (United Kingdom).* [http://www.statistics.gov.uk/cci/nugget.asp?id=719].

Hall, Wiley. "Girls Getting Increasingly Violent." 29 April 2004. *CBS News.* [http://www.cbsnews.com/stories/2004/04/29/national/main614781.shtml]

Lewinsohn, Peter. "Psychosocial functioning of young adults who have experienced and recovered from major depressive disorder during adolescence." *Journal of Abnormal Psychology* 112, no. 3 (2003): 353-63.

Lyons, Linda. "Parents Concerned About School Safety." 17 September 2002. *The Gallup Organization.* [http://www.gallup.com/poll/content/login.aspx?ci=6808].

Muntner, Paul, Jiang He, Jeffery Cutler, Rachel Wildman, and Paul Whelton. "Trends in Blood Pressure among Children and Adolescents." *Journal of the American Medical Association* 291, no. 17 (2004): 2107-13.

# Selected Bibliography

National Institute on Alcohol Abuse and Alcoholism. *Alcohol Alert*. Bethesda, Md.: 1997.

National Institute for Mental Health. *Blueprint for Change: Research on Child and Adolescent Mental Health*. Washington, DC: 2000.

Office of National Drug Control Policy. *National Drug Control Strategy, 2003 Annual Report*. Washington, DC: 2003.

Selye, Hans. *The Stress of Life*. New York: McGraw-Hill Book Company, 1956.

Silverman, J.G. et al. "Dating Violence Against Adolescent Girls and Associated Substance Use, Unhealthy Weight Control, Sexual Risk Behavior, Pregnancy, and Suicidality." *Journal of the American Medical Association* 286, no. 5 (2001): 572-79.

"Smoking Kills: A White Paper on Tobacco." 10 December 1998. Great Britain Department of Health. [http://www.archive.official-documents.co.uk/document/cm41/4177/4177.htm].

Steinberg, Laurence. *You and Your Adolescent*. Revised Edition. New York: Harper Resource, 1997.

"Study: Child Obesity 'Epidemic.'" 24 March 2004. *CBS News*. [http://www.cbsnews.com/stories/2004/04/27/health/main614000.shtml].

"Suicide Among the Young." *Centers for Disease Control*. 2000. [Reported at http://www.save.org/basics/facts.html].

"Teen Stress: How can we help teens cope?" 1999. [http://panic disorder.about.com/library/weekly/aa102799.htm.] Accessed 31 October 2003.

U.S. Department of Health and Human Services. *2000 National Survey on Drug Abuse*. Rockville, Md.: 2001.

U.S. Department of Health and Human Services. *Mental Health: A Report of the Surgeon General*. Rockville, Md.: 1999.

*Youth Violence: A Report of the Surgeon General*. Washington, DC: Department of Health and Human Services, 2001.

## Chapter 2

*Balance*. Ottawa: Human Resources Development Canada, 2003.

Bond, J.T. et al. *National Study of the Changing Workforce*. New York: Families and Work Institute, 2002.

Bonné, Jon. "Are we done with the 40-hour week?" 25 August 2003. *MSNBC*. [http://www.msnbc.msn.com/id/3072426].

Duxbury, L., Higgins, C., & Coghill, D. (2003). *Voices of Canadians: Seeking work-life balance*. Ottawa, ON: Human Resources Development Canada.

Elkind, David. *The Hurried Child: Growing Up Too Fast Too Soon*. Reading, Mass.: Addison-Wesley, 1981.

"Federal Housing Finance Board Reports October Average House Price of $243,756." *Federal Housing Finance Board*. 25 November 2003. [http://www.fhfb.gov/mirs/mirs_press2.htm].

Hickman, Jonathan W. "The Real Tween." 2003. *Entertainment Insiders*. [http://www.einsiders.com/reviews/archives/thirteen.php].

Hymowitz, Kay. *Ready or Not: What Happens When We Treat Children as Small Adults*. San Francisco: Encounter Books, 2000.

Horsman, Karen. Interview with author. January 2004.

Luthar, S.S, and K. D'Avanzo. "Contextual Factors in Substance Use: A Study of Suburban and Inner-City Adolescents." *Development and Psychology* 11, no. 4 (1999): 845-67.

Niesslen, Jennifer. "Living Full-Throttle. Motherhood, Balance, and Another Women's Movement." May 2003. *The Mothers Movement Online*. [http://www.mothersmovement.org/essays/JNeisslein-0305/JNiesslein-0305-1.htm].

Prescott, James. "America's Lost Dream: 'Life, Liberty And The Pursuit Of Happiness.' Current Research and Historical Background on the Origins of Love & Violence." Paper presented to The Association for Prenatal and Perinatal Psychology and Health 10th International Congress. December 2001. Revised August 1, 2002. [http://www.violence.de/prescott/appp/ald.pdf].

"Prevalence of Underage Drinking." January 2004. *Center on Alcohol Marketing and Youth.* [http://camy.org/factsheets/index.php?FactsheetID=5].

Rose, Derek "Kids with Big Allowances Going to Pot." *New York Daily News* (20 August 2003).

"Study Shows Young Generation's Brand-Name Playgrounds." *USA Today* (21 April 2003).

Shatzky, Samantha. "Teens and Sex." *Canada.com.* 22 December 2003. Accessed 29 December 2003.

Singleton, C.J. "Industry Employment and the 1990-91 Recession." *Monthly Labor Review* 116, no. 7 (July 1993).

"Targeting Tweens." *Institute for International Research.* 2002. [http://www.iirusa.com/tweens/]. Accessed 4 December 2003.

# Chapter 3

American Academy of Pediatrics. "Breastfeeding and the Use of Human Milk." *Pediatrics* 115, no. 2 (2005): 496-506.

Belsky, Jay. "Quantity Counts: Amount of Child Care and Children's Socioemotional Development." *Journal of Developmental and Behavioral Pediatrics* 23, no. 3 (2002): 167-70.

Bowlby, John. *Child Care and the Growth of Love.* London: Penguin Books, 1953.

"Breastfeeding Statistics in the United States." *Breastfeeding Basics: Breastfeeding Benefits and Barriers.* 1999. http://www.breastfeeding basics.org/cgi-bin/deliver.cgi/content/Introduction/sta_us.html].

Brooks-Gunn, J., W.J. Han, and J. Waldfogel. "Maternal Employment and Child Cognitive Outcomes in the First Three Years of Life." *Child Development* 73, no. 4 (2002): 1052-72.

Bureau of Labor Statistics, U.S. Department of Labor. "Childcare Workers." 2005. *Occupational Outlook Handbook, 2004-05 Edition.* [http://www.bls.gov/oco/ocos170.htm.].

Carvel, John. "Working Mothers Bad for Children." 14 November 2003. *The Guardian*. [http://www.jbaassoc.demon.co.uk/watch/researchbadforchildren.html].

Clarke-Stewart, K.A. "Infant Day Care: Maligned or Malignant." *American Psychologist* 44, no. 2 (February 1989): 266-73.

Clarke-Stewart, K.A. "Parents' Effects on Children's Development: A Decade of Progress?" *Journal of Applied Developmental Psychology* 9, no. 1 (1988): 41-84.

"Good Pay and Benefits Will Keep Childcare Workers from Fleeing." 9 November 2004. *Canadian Union of Public Employees*. [http://cupe.ca/www/ChildCare/10668].

"Harvard professor clarifies implications of daycare research." *massPSY.com*. August/September 2001. [www.masspsy.com/leading/0109_qu.html].

Hymowitz, Kay. *Liberation's Children: Parent and Kids in a Postmodern Age*. Chicago: Ivan R. Dee, 2003.

Kagan, Jerome. "Temperamental Contributions to Social Behavior." (1988 APA Award Address). *American Psychologist* 44, no. 4 (1989): 668-74.

Leach, Penelope. *Children First: What Society Must Do – and Is Not Doing – for Children Today*. New York: Vintage Books, 1994.

Martens, P. "The Provincial Infant Feeding Study: Results and Implications." Presented at the Baby Friendly Coordinating Committee of Manitoba Meeting, Winnipeg, 2000.

Mordecai, Kim. "Dr. Laura Schlessinger Speaks Out about Parenting." *Sacramento Parent's Monthly* (February 2004). [http://sacramento.parenthood.com/articles.html?article_id=5914&segment=localpub].

Robertson, Brian C. *Daycare Deception: What the Child Care Establishment Isn't Telling Us*. San Francisco: Encounter Books, 2003.

Schlessinger, Laura. *Stupid Things Parents Do To Mess Up Their Kids: Don't Have Them If You Won't Raise Them*. New York: Quill, 2001.

Stuart-Macadam, Patricia, and Katherine A. Dettwyler. *Breastfeeding, Biocultural Perspectives*. New York: de Gruyter, 1995.

Sylva, Kathy, et al. "Effective Provision of Pre-School Education Project." Final Report. Institute of Education, University of London. 24 November 2004. [http://action.web.ca/home/crru/rsrcs_crru_full.shtml?x=70338&AA_EX _Session=63].

U.S. Census Bureau. "Industry Statistics Sampler: NAICS 6244, Child Day Care Services." 2002. [http://www.census.gov/epcd/ec97/industry/E6244.HTM].

Watamura, S.E, B. Donzella, J. Alwin, and M.R. Gunnar. "Morning-to-afternoon Increases in Cortisol Concentrations for Infants and Toddlers at Child Care: Age Differences and Behavioral Correlates." *Child Development* 74, no. 4 (2003): 1006-20.

Whitebook, M., C. Howes, and D. Phillips. *Worthy Work, Unlivable Wages: The National Child Care Staffing Study, 1988-1997*. Washington, D.C.: Center for the Child Care Work Force, 1998.

Williams, P.L., S.M. Innis, and A.M.P. Vogel. "Breastfeeding and Weaning Practices in Vancouver." *Canadian Journal of Public Health* 87, no. 4 (1996): 231-36.

"Working mothers' Link to School Failure." 14 March 2001. *BBC News*. [http://news.bbc.co.uk/1/hi/education/1218905.stm].

# Chapter 4

Amato, Paul, and Alan Booth. *A Generation at Risk: Growing Up in an Era of Family Upheaval*. Boston: Harvard University Press, 1997.

Bankenhorn, David. *Fatherless America: Confronting Our Most Urgent Social Problem*. New York: Perennial, 1996.

Benard, B. *Fostering Resiliency in Kids: Protective Factors in the Family, School, and Community*. Portland, Or: Northwest Regional Educational Laboratory, Western Regional Center for Drug Free Schools and Communities, 1991.

Dr. Daly, Kerry. Interview with author, January 2004.

Dixon, Marlene. "Why Women's Liberation?" *Ramparts* 8 (December 1969).

Duignan, Molly. "The Effect of Divorce on Kids." *UWO Gazette* 94, no. 40 (2000).

Fagan, P.F., and R. Rector. *The Effects of Divorce on America*. Washington, D.C.: Heritage Foundation, 2000.

Gordon, Linda. "Functions of the Family." *WOMEN: A Journal of Liberation* (1969).

Gottman, John M. *The Seven Principles for Making Marriage Work: A Practical Guide from the Country's Foremost Relationship Expert*. New York: Three Rivers Press, 2000.

Marston, Stephanie. *The Divorced Parent: Success Strategies for Raising Your Children After Separation*. New York: Pocket Books, 1994.

McGraw, Phil. *Relationship Rescue: A Seven-Step Strategy for Reconnecting with Your Partner*. New York: Hyperion, 2000.

Millett, Kate. *Sexual Politics*. New York: Granada Publishing, 1969.

Waite, Linda et. al. *Does Divorce Make People Happy: Findings from a Study of Unhappy Marriages*. New York: Institute for Family Values, 2002.

Wallerstein, J., J.M. Lewis, and S. Blakeslee. *The Unexpected Legacy of Divorce*. New York: Hyperion, 2000.

Werner, Emmy E., and Ruth S. Smith. *Overcoming the Odds: High Risk Children from Birth to Adulthood*. Ithaca, NY: Cornell University Press, 1992.

Whitehead, Barbara Dafoe. *The Divorce Culture: Rethinking Our Commitments to Marriage and Family*. New York: Vintage Books, 1996.

# Chapter 5

Borst, John. "Parenting as Product Development." April 2002. *The Social Edge.com*. [http://www.thesocialedge.com/archives/other/2commentary-apr2002.htm].

Doherty, W.J. *Take Back Your Kids: Confident Parenting in Turbulent Times*. Notre Dame, In.: Sorin Books, 2000.

Greene, Jay and Greg Forster. "Public High School Graduation and College Readiness Rates in the United States."*Manhattan Institute for Policy Research*. Education Working Paper 3 (September 2003). [http://www.manhattan-institute.org/html/ewp_03.htm].

Healy, Jane. *Endangered Minds: Why Children Don't Think And What We Can Do About It*. New York: Simon & Schuster, 1999.

Hofferth, Sandra L., and John F. Sandberg. "How American Children Spend Their Time." *Journal of Marriage and the Family* 63, no. 2 (2001): 295-308

Luthar, S.S., and B.E. Becker. "Privileged but Pressured: A Study of Affluent Youth." *Child Development* 73, no. 5 (2002.): 1593-610.

"New Book Describes the State of the Church in 2002." 4 June 2002. *The Barna Group*. [http://www.barna.org/FlexPage.aspx?Page= BarnaUpdate&BarnaUpdateID=114].

Simpson, Alan. "The Value of School Recess and Outdoor Play." 2004. *National Association for the Education of Young Children*. [http://www.naeyc.org/ece/1998/08.asp].

"Talking With Teens: The YMCA Parent and Teen Survey Final Report." [www.ymca.net/presrm/research/teensurvey.htm].

"The Lost Children of Rockdale County." *PBS Frontline*. 1999. [http://www.pbs.org/wgbh/pages/frontline/shows/georgia/ interviews/sterk.html].

# Chapter 6

Adlaf, E.M., A. Paglia, and J.H. Beitchman. *The Mental Health and Well-Being of Ontario Students 1991-2001*. Toronto: Centre for Addiction and Mental Health, 2001.

Canadian Centre for Justice Statistics. *Children and Youth in Canada*. Ottawa: Statistics Canada, 2001.

Cornwall, Claudia. "Parents, Your Marks Are In." *Readers Digest* (June 2004).

"Discipline: A Parent's Guide." 2005. *National PTA*. [http://www.pta.org/parentinvolvement/helpchild/disc.asp].

Geelan, D.R. *Falling Through The Cracks: A Summary of What We Heard About Teaching and Learning Conditions in Alberta Schools*. Edmonton, Alta: Alberta Teachers' Association, 2002.

Ginott, Haim. *Between Parent & Child: New Solutions to Old Problems*. New York: The Macmillan Company, 1965.

Hart, Louise. *The Winning Family: Increasing Self-Esteem in Your Children and Yourself*. New York: Dodd, Mead & Company, 1987.

Henderson, Paul. *A Snapshot of What Parents Think About Schooling in New Zealand*. Auckland, New Zealand: Maxim Institute, 2004.

Hymowitz, Kay. *Liberation's Children: Parents and Kids in a Postmodern Age*. Chicago: Ivan R. Dee, 2003

Kenny, William. "Rice to Pols: Discipline in the Schools is Troubling." 28 August 2002. *Northeast Times*. [http://www.northeasttimes.com/2002/0828/discipline.html].

Knight, Bob. "Cities say curfews cut youth crime." *The Morning News* (28 February 2000).

Kuczynski, Leon. Interview with author. January 2004.

Lollis, S. "Conceptualizing the Influence of the Past and Future in Present Parent-Child Relationships." In *Handbook of Dynamics in Parent-Child Relations*. Ed. L. Kuczynski. Thousand Oaks, CA: Sage, 2003.

Mamen, Maggie. *The Pampered Child Syndrome: How To Recognize It, How To Manage It, And How To Avoid It*. Ottawa: Creative Bound, 2004.

Nansel, Tonja R., et al. "Bullying Behaviors Among US Youth: Prevalence and Association With Psychosocial Adjustment." *Journal of the American Medical Association* 285 (2001): 2094-100.

Nord, Christine Winquist. "Issue Brief: Students Do Better When Their Fathers Are Involved at School (NCES 98121)." Washington, D.C.: National Center for Education Statistics, 1998.

"Olweus Bullying Prevention Program." 22 March 2005. [http://www.clemson.edu/olweus/index.html]

Public Agenda. *Teaching Interrupted: Do Discipline Policies in Today's Public Schools Foster the Common Good?* New York: May 2004.

Schneider, William J., Timothy A. Cavell, Jan N. Hughes. "A Sense of Containment: Potential Moderator of the Relation between Parenting Practices and Children's Externalizing Behaviors." *Development and Psychopathology* 15, no. 1 (March 2003): 95-117.

"School Discipline – What's to be done?" *BBC News*. 6 June 2001. [http://news.bbc.co.uk/vote2001/hi/english/talking_point/newsid_12200 00/1220670.stm. ]. Accessed June 2001.

Spock, Benjamin. *The Common Sense Book of Baby & Child Care*. New York: Duell, Sloan & Pierce, 1946.

Trumbull, H. Clay. *Hints on Child Training*. Philadelphia: John D. Wattles, 1891.

Valentine, C.W. *The Difficult Child and the Problem of Discipline*. London: Methuen & Co., 1940.

# Chapter 7

American Academy of Pediatrics. "Joint Statement on the Impact of Entertainment Violence on Children." 26 July 2000.

[http://www.aap.org/advocacy/releases/jstmtevc.htm].

Anderson, C.A., and B.J. Bushman. "Effects of Violent Games on Aggressive Behavior, Aggressive Cognition, Aggressive Affect, Physiological Arousal, and Prosocial Behavior: A Meta-Analytic Review of the Scientific Literature." *Psychological Science* 12 (2001): 353-59.

Anderson, C.A., N.L. Carnagey, and J. Eubanks. "Exposure to Violent Media: The Effects of Songs with Violent Lyrics on Aggressive Thoughts and Feelings." *Journal of Personality and Social Psychology* 84, no. 5 (2003): 960-71.

Bergen, D., and D. Mauer. "Symbolic Play, Phonological Awareness, and Literacy Skills at Three Age Levels." In *Play and Literacy in Early Childhood: Research from Multiple Perspectives*. Ed. K. A. Roskos and J.F. Christie. Mahwah, NJ: Lawrence Erlbaum Associates, 2000.

Bushman, B.J., and C.A. Anderson. "Media violence and the American public: Scientific facts versus media misinformation." *American Psychologist* 56 (2001): 477-89.

Canadian Teachers Federation. *Kids' Take on Media - Full Report.* Ottawa: 2003.

Center for Communication and Social Policy, University of California, Santa Barbara. *National Television Violence Study 3.* Thousand Oaks, CA: Sage, 1998.

Children Now. *Fair Play? Violence, Gender and Race in Video Games.* Oakland: December 2001.

Christakis, D.A., and F.J. Zimmerman. "Does Children's Watching of Television Cause Attention Problems? Retesting the Hypothesis in a Danish Cohort." *Pediatrics* 114 (2004): 1373-74.

Collins, R.L. et al. "Watching sex on television predicts adolescent initiation of sexual behavior." *Pediatrics* 114, no. 3 (2004): 280-289.

Ervin-Tripp, S. "Play in Language Development." In *Play and the Social Context of Development in Early Care and Education.* Ed. B. Scales, M. Almy, A. Nicolopoulou, and S. Ervin-Tripp. New York: Teachers College Press, 1991.

"Few Parents Use V-Chip to Block TV Sex and Violence." 24 July 2001. *Kaiser Family Foundation.* [http://www.kff.org/entmedia/3158-V-Chip -release.cf].

Gentile, D.A., and C.A. Anderson. "Violent Video Games: The Newest Media Violence Hazard." In *Media Violence and Children.* Ed. D.A. Gentile. Westport, Ct.: Praeger Publishing, 2003.

Gentile, D.A., and D.A. Walsh. "A Normative Study of Family Media Habits." *Applied Developmental Psychology* 23 (2002): 157-78.

Gentile, D.A., et al. "The Effects of Violent Video Game Habits on Adolescent Hostility, Aggressive Behaviors, and School Performance." *Journal of Adolescence* 27 (2004): 5-22.

Grier, Sonja. "The Federal Trade Commission's Report on the Marketing of Violent Entertainment to Youths: Developing Policy-Tuned Research." *Journal of Public Policy and Marketing* 20, no. 1 (Spring 2001): 123-32.

Huesman, L.R., and L.D. Eron. *Television and the Aggressive Child: A Cross-National Comparison.* Hillsdale, N.J.: Lawrence Erlbaum, 1986.

Krahé, B., and I. Möller. "Playing Violent Electronic Games, Hostile Attributional Style, and Aggression-related Norms in German Adolescents." *Journal of Adolescence* 27 (2004): 53-69.

MacBeth, Tannis, ed. *Tuning Into Young Viewers*. Newbury Park, CA: Sage Publications, 1996.

Newman, L.S. "Intentional Versus Unintentional Memory in Young Children: Remembering Versus Playing." *Journal of Experimental Child Psychology* 50 (1990): 243-58.

Roberts, D.F., et al. *Kids and Media @ the New Millennium*. Menlo Park, CA: Kaiser Family Foundation, 1999.

Singer, D.G., and J, Singer. *The House of Make-Believe*. Cambridge: Harvard University Press, 1990.

Stein, A.H., and L.K. Friedrich. "Television Content and Young Children's Behavior." In *Television and Social Behavior*. Vol. 2. Ed. J.P. Murray, E.A. Rubinstein, and G.A. Comstock. Washington, DC: United States Government Printing Office, 1972.

"Television a Worrisome Old Friend." 2002. *Public Agenda Online*. [http://www.publicagenda.org/specials/parents/parents2.htm].

Thompson, K.M., and F. Yokota. "Violence, Sex, and Profanity in Films: Correlation of Movie Ratings with Content." *Medscape General Medicine* 6, no. 3 (13 July 2004).

Victoria Rideout. *Parents, Media and Public Policy: A Kaiser Family Foundation Survey*. Menlo Park, CA: Kaiser Family Foundation, 2004.

"Violence." 1992. *Teen Health and the Media*. [www.depts.washington.edu/thmedia/view.cgi?section=violence].

# Chapter 8

"Body Image and Nutrition." 1992. *Teen Health and the Media*. [http://depts.washington.edu/thmedia/view.cgi?section=bodyimage].

Camargo, Carlos. "Chubby Kids May Be at Greater Risk for Asthma." *New York Times* (27 April 1999).

Center for Alcohol Marketing and Youth. "Television Alcohol Ads Bombarding Teens Continue to Rise." 12 October 2004.

Collins, M.E. "Body Figure Perceptions and Preferences Among Pre-adolescent Children." *International Journal of Eating Disorders* (1991): 199-208.

Dreyfuss, Ira. "Inactivity Blamed for Teens' Weight Gains." *The Associated Press* (13 May 2003).

Field, Alison E., et al. "Exposure to the Mass Media and Weight Concerns Among Girls." *Pediatrics* 103, no. 3 (March 1999): e36 (electronic article). [http://pediatrics.aappublications.org/cgi/content/full/103/3/e36].

Janssen, I., W. Craig, W.F. Boyce, and W. Pickett. "Associations Between Overweight and Obesity With Bullying Behaviors in School-Aged Children." *Pediatrics* 113 (2004): 1187-94.

Jean Holzgang. "Facts on Body and Image." April 14, 2000. *Just Think Foundation*. [http://www.justthink.org/bipfact.html].

Ladwig, K.H., B. Marten-Mittag, H. Löwel, A. Döring, and W. Koenig. "Influence of depressive mood on the association of CRP and obesity in 3205 middle aged healthy men." *Brain, Behavior and Immunity* 17, no. 4 (2003): 268-75.

Latner, J.D., and A.J. Stunkard. "Getting Worse: The Stigmatization of Obese Children." *Obesity Research* 11 (2003): 452-56

MacPherson, Karen. "Developmental Experts Say Children Suffer Due to Lack of Unstructured Play." *Pittsburgh Post-Gazette* (1 October 2002).

Mellin, L., S. McNutt, Y. Hu, G.B. Schreiber, P. Crawford, and E. Obarzanek. "A Longitudinal Study of the Dietary Practices of Black and White Girls 9 and 10 Years Old at Enrollment: The NHLBI Growth and Health Study." *Journal of Adolescent Health* (1991): 27-37.

Owens, T., and S. Hofferth, eds. *Children at the Millennium: Where Have We Come From, Where are We Going? Advances in Life Course Research.* New York: Elsevier Science, 2001.

Raitakari, Olli T., et al. "Cardiovascular Risk Factors in Childhood and Carotid Artery Intima-Media Thickness in Adulthood: The

Cardiovascular Risk in Young Finns Study." *Journal of the American Medical Association* 290 (2003): 2277–83.

Scwartz, Jon. "High Death Rate Lingers Behind Fun Facade of Pro Wrestling." *USA Today* (12 March 2004)

Smith, K.A., C.G. Fairburn, and P.J. Cowen. "Symptomatic Relapse in Bulimia Nervosa Following Acute Tryptophan Depletion." *Archives of General Psychiatry* 56 (1999): 171-76.

Squires, Sally. "Obesity-Linked Diabetes Rising in Children Experts Attending Agriculture Dept. Forum Call for New Strategies to Reverse Trend." *Washington Post* (3 November 1998).

"Statistics: How Many People Have Eating Disorders?" November 2004. *Anorexia Nervosa and Related Eating Disorders, Inc.* [http://www.anred.com/stats.html.]

Tantisira, K.G., and S.T. Weiss. "Complex Interactions in Complex Traits: Obesity and Asthma." *Thorax* 56 (2001): 64-74.

Thompson, Elizabeth. "Teens Mirror Parents with Lifestyle Choices." *Calgary Herald* (November 2003).

Tremblay, M.S., P.T. Katzmarzyk, and J.D. Willms. "Temporal Trends in Overweight and Obesity in Canada, 1981-1996." *International Journal of Obesity* 26, no. 4 (1999): 538-43.

Weiss, Ram, et al. "Obesity and the Metabolic Syndrome in Children and Adolescents." *New England Journal of Medicine* 350 (2004): 2362-74.

Woo, Kam S., et al. "Effects of Diet and Exercise on Obesity-Related Vascular Dysfunction in Children." *Circulation* 109 (2004): 1981-86.

Zimmerman, Sara. "Let Them Play." *National Post* (2 September 2003).

# Index

# Index